THE "DIS-EASE" IS THE CURE

FROM MIND-OVER-SOUL TO SOUL-OVER-MIND

A BETTER WAY TO MIND YOUR BUSINESS

By Leonard Burg

"Far more indispensable than food for the physical body is spiritual nourishment for the soul. One can do without food for a considerable time, but a [hu]man of the spirit cannot exist for a single second without spiritual nourishment."[1]

INNERSPIRE

PRESS

Printed in the United States of America.

ISBN-13: 978-1-7347356-0-4

Innerspire Press
626 Riverside Dr, Suite 4-O, New York, NY 10031

TABLE OF CONTENTS

FOREWORD

Who I am and Why I, Leonard Burg, Wrote This Book About DIS-EASE

The crafting of this book—*THE "DIS-EASE" is the Cure; From Mind-Over-Soul to Soul-Over-Mind; A Better Way to Mind Your Business*—is the culmination of a lifetime of experiences, study, practice, and an ongoing search for healing, spiritual fulfillment, and self-mastery, that form the basis of my work as a Soul Therapist.

The fruits of this quest have guided me in realizing that estrangement from the universal spiritual dimension of life has been a major missing link in humanity, dominated by the mind and ego, being able to realize true inner peace, fulfillment, and alleviation of suffering, in spite of achieving some measure of material fame, fortune, or development.

This alienation is a root causal factor of what I call DIS-EASE: upset in mind, body, and social circumstances. It is something that we have all faced in one way or another—as individuals, in relationships, in businesses or organizations; and in a social or global context. It manifests as physical disease, estrangement and breakups in relationships, wars, conflicts, poverty and environmental degradation. In making it my business to study DIS-EASE, I have discovered that it is an effort of the life force in organisms to direct it towards healing and remediation, if it is cooperated with rather than simply suppressed. I recollect that MY personal relationship with DIS-EASE began with parental abandonment.

ABANDONMENT: Left in the Lurch on the Road Toward Self-Mastery

We started out as a loving, intact nuclear family, with a father we idolized and a mother we adored. But then, in spite of the love that both parents had for us, circumstances led to each, at one time or another, breaking away from their children. So, my early life began with a recovery from parental abandonment, first by my mother, then my father.

As helpless babes, then minors, we are dependent on our parents to guide us in becoming independent, self-sufficient adults, living and working in harmony with self and others, and sharing our gifts with the world. **In effect, our parents are our first "masters," and we are their apprentices.** In retrospect, their leaving temporarily made me feel robbed of an early apprentice-ship with mastership. However, it ultimately was a factor that propelled me toward self-mastery.

Abandonment makes you squarely face the challenge of mastering yourself. And you learn major lessons in the course of facing challenges. In the process, **if you are wise, you learn to forgive, to take responsibility, and to seek guidance from mentorship and mastership** in extended family, friends, and in every field of endeavor, especially from God within, as you navigate life's waters. I have, and it is what has kept me afloat, propelling forward; it has enabled me to live a useful life of service to others in spite of bouts with DIS-EASE. It wasn't until later in life that I grasped what had driven my mother, Anne Burg, and my father, Leonard Burg, Sr., to at times abandon us, which, for all of us were heart-wrenching upheavals.

Driven to Abandonment

I was seven years old when my mother suddenly up and left my father, me, and my four siblings (Allynne, Joan, Jennifer, and Rodney) for reasons we would only find out later. She eventually revealed what happened. She said that one day my father, who had a history of alcohol abuse, came home half-drunk, sat her down, and put a gun on the table. He accused her of having an affair when hanging out with her girlfriends on the other side of the housing projects where we lived in lower Manhattan, NY. So, she fled, in fear of her life. As a result, it was my older sister Allynne who fortunately played a major role in looking after us in our early youth. Her loving, motherly support and caring has continued selflessly over the course of her life.

And then my father disappeared when I was eleven years old. He dropped off my younger brother and me with our maternal grandparents, "Grand-mommy and Beebo" (who got that name as my older sister tried to say we're going to see the "people.") The plan was for us to spend the summer with them in White Plains—a suburb of New York City. Dad also dropped off my three sisters at a summer camp in upstate NY. Dad was supposed to pick us all up when school started and move us to a new house in Connecticut in a neighboring suburb. However, without a word, he never showed up. Fortunately, through my maternal grandparents, we had maintained a relationship with my mother. She and her boyfriend, Pascal Goodman (who served as a loving surrogate father), had to come get us and move us all to a small tenement apartment in the Bronx, NY. Eventually, however, I did get some insight into why my father had disappeared.

Seven years after abandoning us, he resurfaced. We had hunted him down when a childhood ailment reappeared in my younger brother. By then, my father had become a truck driver. Partly out of guilt, no doubt, he offered to pay my way to college—to New York University (NYU)—a dream for himself that he had failed to materialize. One day, after a sit-down with him and sharing a few marijuana joints, he revealed the pain and agony he had suffered as his life fell apart and his dreams were dashed, unable to support himself or keep his family together. Whereas he had once made a lucrative living hanging wallpaper in the homes of the well-to-do, he had to leave that profession because he became severely allergic to the wall painting that invariably preceded the paper hanging.

Fortunately for me, it was through therapy and spiritual teachings that, over time, I began to really understand the impact that the DIS-EASE of abandonment had had on me, and its relationship to my eventual healing and resurrection. In spite of it all, with the loving help of friends, extended family, and teachers of all persuasions, I recognized that I was being prepared for a journey toward self-mastery, that nothing happened to me by accident, that even though others may deliver the blow, that I am the sower of the seeds that bear fruit in my life and that my blessed father and mother were the channel through which I was given this great gift of life and the opportunity to realize my divinity. I had to realize that the DIS-EASE in my life has not itself been the enemy to beat, but had been designed to awaken me to who I really am.

> **I had to realize that the DIS-EASE in my life has not itself been the enemy to beat, but had been designed to awaken me to who I really am.**

Education and Rebellion

Much of my personal enlightenment accelerated when I finally made it to college at NYU between 1967 and 1971. It was then that I experienced social/political DIS-EASE. The decade of the '60s was a time of upheaval in the United States. Malcolm X, a fierce black leader, had been assassinated, as had been the Reverend Dr. Martin Luther King, Jr., President John F. Kennedy, and his brother, Robert Kennedy. And, as I learned later, there had systematically been assassinations and assaults on several dynamic leaders on the African continent. As I delved deeper into my black African identity, I became increasingly alienated, distressed, and angry about the oppression visited upon African peoples.

In the wake of the assassinations and oppressive conditions in predominantly black and urban communities, there were intermittent rebellions (called "riots" by the media) in cities across the country. I was knee-deep in the middle of the campus rebellions as a black student leader at NYU. In fact, during one demonstration, I entered the university's administration building with a gallon of gasoline strapped to my shoulder, ready to blow the place up. But it hit me. Why am I doing this? Is this who I am? I couldn't answer for sure. So, instead, I turned on the water pumps and flooded the place.

In retrospect, it might have helped in my college years to have sought or taken advantage of the mastership of a mentor other than from my peers who, like me, were young, headstrong, and preoccupied with engaging in struggle. Many of us actually joked that if the revolution were to take place immediately, we wouldn't want to be under the rulership of some of the activists we were exposed to in the limelight of the movement because of their own brand of authoritarianism and lack of ethics.

I left NYU in 1971 without graduating, having spent more time out of class than in. However, I had worked one summer as a field representative and motivation achievement trainer in an internship program for the National Urban League (N.U.L.), a major civil rights organization in the USA, with over 100 local affiliates throughout the country. Luckily, Mr. Ron Brown, a leader in the organization (and eventual Secretary of Commerce under President Clinton), had taken notice of my activism. So, they hired me as co-director of Youth and Student Affairs. Even so, by this time I was burnt out and stressed from my tumultuous struggles at NYU. What made it worse was my steady diet of the "three Ws:" wine, women, and weed (marijuana), with a touch of LSD and cocaine.

Clearly, in spite of my black consciousness, I still wasn't clear about my identity. I was still in a DIS-EASED state, trying to escape, but from what and to where? This reminds me of the simple lesson given by two great icons:

> The great U.S. boxer, Joe Louis, once said, "You can run, but you can't hide."

> And the great musician Bob Marley sang, "Ya running and ya running and ya running away... But ya can't run away from yourself."

True, that. Eventually, I had to look within and find myself.

Who am I?

By the time I left NYU and joined the N.U.L., I was suffering from chronic respiratory conditions and skin problems. My acne-scarred face looked to me like the craters of the moon or the rugged skin of an alligator. On top of that, I was devastated by a failed love affair, even though for the first time in my life I had openly borne my heart and expressed my love for another human being. On top of that, I was not fulfilled or happy sitting behind a desk at the N.U.L. So, in 1973, I quit my well-paying job there in order to try and find myself.

I began by getting an expensive, comprehensive physical exam, including an EKG, urine and blood tests, and the like. Afterwards, I was stunned, flabbergasted, and incredulous when they told me that I was in perfect health. Fortunately, I was wise enough to not blindly accept that prognosis. By then, however, my knowledge of alternative or holistic health was limited. Ironically, a good friend at the N.U.L. Ms. Ayesha Grice, had dropped off a copy of the book, *Rational Fasting* by Arnold Ehret on my desk shortly before I left. It was to play a big part in my resurrection as I was to later learn that **toxins that don't exit through the normal channels of elimination, the bowels and the urinary tract, will come out through the skin. And this can psychosomatically reveal the insecurities we have about self, as if this outer mask represents who we really are in essence.** Eventually this did make me look more closely at myself.

A Spiritual Bomb is Detonated

It was upon leaving the N.U.L. in 1973 that a spiritual explosion ignited within me. I became an avid seeker on the spiritual path in order to answer the questions: who am I, why am I here, what am I supposed to be doing, and what is my true identity and destiny in life? So, I enrolled in "UCLA;" not the school in California, but the "University at the Corner of Lenox Avenue" in Harlem, NY—a spiritual bookstore owned by a Mr. Kanya Kekumba. It attracted all the more advanced practitioners of spirituality and holism in the area. Even the band "Earth, Wind, and Fire" visited there at times for their spiritual nourishment.

That year I began classes at a Rosicrucian spiritual Center on "Striver's Row," a brownstone-lined street on 138th street in Harlem, NY. The teacher was Rogelio Straughn (aka Ra Un Nefer Amen), who, in the next 40+ years came to be renowned as Shekem Ur Shekem, leader of the Ausar Auset Society, an African- and Kemetic- (aka Egyptian) oriented spiritual community. I was one of the first to teach an astrology class for him. It was then that his teaching blessed me with what was an awe-inspiring realization:

> **That I am, in essence, not this body/mind, but a divine immortal spirit—my true "Self"—that inhabits this body, and this divine spirit in me has infinite potential and ability to express itself.**

Thereafter, life's goal for me became first-hand spiritual experience, self-mastery, and realizing my divinity. In route to that higher goal, I began to seriously explore and experience periodic fasting (cleaning out my Divine Temple—see the appendix). I started with a seven-day water fast, which I stuck to even though visions of pork chops titillated my mind. **Fasting was a curative way of simulating DIS-EASE in order to facilitate the organism healing itself.**

First, I became a fruitarian, then a vegetarian. At the time, it scared my mother, because, in the process, my weight dropped to 130 pounds before it picked up again. She would worriedly tell me, "You have that lean and hungry look." And my grandfather, Beebo, who would generally accept my lifestyle changes, questioned this vegetarian thing by incredulously asking, "You mean you don't eat chicken?" Like many southern descendants, we had eaten fried chicken almost every Sunday.

I had become a vegetarian, not just for health or environmental sustainability reasons, but because of the possible stunting of my spiritual growth due to the killing of animals for food and interrupting the life cycle of their souls. In the process, as I deepened my exploration of spirituality and holism, I also became a practitioner of acupressure massage and holistic health education through studying and/or experiencing a variety of holistic modalities: the Kabbalah—a Jewish mystery system, homeopathy, occultism, the oracles of I Ching and Tarot, Yoga, Tai Chi, religious scriptures, mysticism, etc. Above all, I saw myself as a seeker.

Fatherhood and Paying it Forward

During the early years of my spiritual journey in the 1970s and '80s, I also worked at day jobs consulting and directing community programs, and counseling youths in Harlem, NY while operating a holistic practice at the same time. In 1975, I moved in with a woman, Moteesala (aka Elaine Hill), when living with my cousin Surya in the Bronx. (He had taken me under his wing like a big brother during my high school years after I had moved in with my maternal grandparents to take some of the load off my mother.) Earlier, I had witnessed Moteesala's sixteen-year-old son, Jerome, blithefully riding around in her car, unbeknownst to her. Upon my informing her of this, we began to see each other. For two years, we spent much of the time nurturing Jerome and Moteesala's older daughter Debbie—from the streets to enrollment in college. Sadly, however, that's when Moteesala and I came face-to-face with each other and realized that we had not really resolved some issues in our relationship.

It was then that I had my first experience with psychotherapy. I was working at the time with a Mr. Bill Burnes administering a program that brought hundreds of college, high school, and elementary school students and youths, including Jerome and Debbie, on the campus of City College in Harlem, NY for remedial programs and camps. Bill definitely exhibited mastership, even with having had just a limited secondary school education. **In opening up to the therapist, I realized that I was prone toward being a savior rather than really paying attention to what I felt and needed.** This led to Moteesala and I parting ways after two years of living together. In retrospect, I value the lessons I learned in my relationship with her. She sadly passed away years later. However, I remain happily in contact with her/my daughter Debbie (I refuse to use the prefix "step"). I realize that my relationship with Moteesala and the children was an opportunity to give back what had been given to me when my mother's boyfriend took me and my four siblings in and showed us the love and devotion for which our souls had thirsted.

The Power of Dialogue

In working and interacting with Harlem youths, being introduced to the world of conventional psychotherapy, and continuing my studies into the influence of mind and spirit on physical conditions, I was gaining a greater appreciation of the need to open up and be truthful about what was going on inside of me in relation to self and others. **Gradually, I realized that the individuals and organizations I had "treated" in my consulting and holistic practice benefitted as much from soul-searching, interactive dialogue as they had from various "hands-on" organizational development or holistic healing modalities.**

In fact, in studying Homeopathy, I learned that just listening to and dialoguing with clients can ignite the healing process. All of this helped form the basis of the methodology of Soul Therapy as a Holistic treatment, which later was further enriched when meeting some world-class, metaphysically-conscious psychotherapists from Brazil.

I remember one example of the power of dialogue in treating my massage clients. They would open up and talk while I worked on them at Daya Associates - Nu Age Center of Harlem, a holistic health center I worked out of in the 1980s and '90s. After sending clients on to get colonic irrigations at the same center to clean out their intestines, I was intrigued when the founder and head colon therapist/yoga maestra, Daya Quander (aka Anjupita Virimo) told me that my clients dumped twice as many toxins as people who came just to get colonics.

I had met Daya in 1973 at Aquarius House, a yoga center she operated in a brownstone building on 148th street in the Sugar Hill section of Harlem. She was to play a pivotal role in my life, in developing a spiritually based holistic practice. My deeper understanding of DIS-EASE was rapidly forming.

The DIS-EASE is the Cure

Through my holistic and spiritual experiences and studies, I began to realize that DIS-EASE, or upsetting symptoms, problems, and germs or conflicts are the spirit's attempt to rid the organism—individual or social—of morbific or toxic matter; in other words, the organism heals itself, to the extent possible, if one cooperates with it and "treats" it with the kind of "food" that sustains life, even if some "emergency medicine" or temporary suppressive professional interventions are necessary. And most profoundly of all, **I learned that the greatest vital, life-giving "food" is truth and consciousness—the key to nourishing the spirit.**

Later, I was to learn from enlightened spiritual masters that what I call DIS-EASE, far from being the enemy, is what makes us pay attention to what is really going on inside of us that we may be blind to; that **it may take poverty, ill health or humiliation (DIS-EASE), to bring us to our knees, that we need stop limiting our focus to the material, but look more toward a higher purpose in life** by reaching "in" to the divine for spiritual guidance and healing. One might believe that it is enough to just be "religious," to pray and go to church, mosque, synagogue, or temple inside. However, I was to learn that this alone does not necessarily confer first-hand experience of the divine, in spite of their sometimes beautiful but symbolic rites and rituals. Rather I learned that **the real house of worship is this human body, which the Most High has gifted us.**

> **Through my holistic and spiritual experiences and studies, I began to realize that DIS-EASE, or upsetting symptoms, problems, and germs or conflicts are the spirit's attempt to rid the organism—individual or social—of morbific or toxic matter; in other words, the organism heals itself, to the extent possible**

<u>Journey from Conventional Religion to Global Spirituality and
Consciousness</u>

In growing up, I had been exposed to Presbyterianism and that old-time Southern Baptist religion. Later in my spiritual quest, during the late 1970s and early '80s, I was baptized in a Pentecostal church where I witnessed the speaking of tongues and mediumship. For me, at the time, this seemed closer to actual spiritual experience than the dry, polite polemics and reading of scriptures. I had already spent several years studying traditional African religion, which took spirit possession and ancestral worship to another level. However, my spirit was leading me to explore the eternal dimensions beyond the mortal realms of ancestors and angels after later being exposed to several living saints and spiritual teachers.

One Indian mystic told a related story about a spiritual seeker, Arjuna, whose son was killed in a war while Arjuna was away fighting in another area. Arjuna was despondent because he had not had a chance to say goodbye to his son. So, he begged his spiritual guide, Krishna, to take him up into the spiritual realms to say a final goodbye to his son. Krishna was reluctant, but finally agreed and took Arjuna up into the spiritual realms, in meditation, to meet the spirit who had been his son. Upon arrival, his "son" asked why Arjuna had come there and who was it that he wanted to talk to. Because, said the spirit, in other lives I have been your mother, your father, your son, your daughter, etc. This reinforced in me the desire to go beyond lineage and the realms of ancestral spirits to the throne of our one common ancestor, the Supreme Being.

In the process of continuing my spiritual studies, I did not forsake the religious teachings I had been exposed to. In fact, I was to gain even more appreciation of the underlying universality and core principles of Christianity, other religions, and diverse spiritual teachings (and their saviors and redeemers). As I progressed, spiritual masters—including so-called "Gurus", the word of which means "giver of light"—were to teach me that **we are attracted to our early religious experiences and teachers by our destiny, and it is often a preparation or sowing of the seed and tilling of the soil, for deeper spiritual teachings and**

experience. Here's how the great musician Carlos Santana said it in his biography, "The Universal Tone":

> "The reason for gurus is that you can't do it by yourself all the time—definitely not at the beginning. You need someone else to hold up the light so you can see where you're going on your new road. A true guru is someone who brings light and is a dispeller of darkness. Jesus was a guru. Sometimes, it's nothing that gurus say or do but how they change things by their presence. If we all could just tell ourselves, over and over, that the spark of the divine in us will triumph over our feet of clay—done. There'd be no need for gurus or guides. If only it were that easy."[2]

Ultimately, this led me on a spiritual journey from the streets of Harlem, NY to Africa, Europe, India, and Brazil where I met and studied at the feet of universally-minded indigenous holistic healers, saints, spiritual masters, and highly-evolved teachers and practitioners in the sciences of body and mind. My international journeys began not long after my first formal or "legal" marriage to Ms. Sydnade Jackson in 1982. We spent ten years together seeking on the spiritual path. During that period, we had two children, Kemikaa and Kopavi. And for a few years, we also took care of her niece, Mashon, and her nephew, Maurice (who later became a Harvard educated psychiatrist). Once again, I had been given the opportunity to pay it forward, to serve youths in need just like I had been served by so many extended family and friends when separated from my parents.

A Spiritual Renaissance - From Harlem to the Bush

The 1970s and 1980s was a time of holistic and spiritual renaissance in Harlem, NY. Just before marrying Sydnade, I was initiated by an Indian master, Sri Soami Divyanand Ji Maharaj in my home in the fall of 1982. We met after I offered my place as a site for His lecture and meditation during His tour of the U.S. However, after being initiated, I temporarily lost touch with

Him because, at the time, I didn't really grasp the profundity of the spiritual path He practiced, "The Science of the Soul." I, like many black people, had a conditioned response to the word "master." You say "master," I think "slave." But I was soon to come out of that way of thinking as I began to understand what self-mastery is all about and how **from time immemorial there have been "masters" and "apprentices" in all fields.** Even today, we run to get our master's degree, yielding to one who has already achieved that status.

Soami Divyanand and I were to eventually reunite at his spiritual center in Germany in 1992, after the death of my mother. In the interim, I was to meet several other spiritual masters recognized in their milieu as saints or mystics and spent ten years working with a spiritual community: Sserulanda Nsulo Y'Obulamu Spiritual Foundation, based in Uganda, East Africa.

It was through a Ms. Janet Feldman, a wealthy spiritual seeker, that I had come in contact with Sserulanda. She and I had joined forces in the early 1980s to organize a city-wide monthly meditation and spiritual group for diverse spiritual seekers. (In one of our meetings, we put Mr. Walter Beebe, founder of the famous *Open Center* in New York City, in a meditation and healing circle. He was having problems closing on the deal to find a home for the center. I can't say that our circle was a prime factor in clearing the way, but I'm sure it helped.) Janet was familiar with many prominent figures in United Nations circles. One of them was former UN Assistant Secretary-General, Robert Muller.

It just so happened that Janet had met two travelers representing the spiritual master and founder of Sserulanda, Bambi Baaba. They were trying to connect with Muller in their efforts to help Bambi Baaba build an eco-friendly spiritual city there in Uganda that they considered to be a Cosmic Focal Point near Lake Victoria, the largest lake in the world, and the source of the Nile River.

So, Janet decided to invite my wife and me to dinner at her penthouse apartment in the Chelsea neighborhood of Manhattan, NY, to meet Noella (Nabeewa) Mcnicoll and Bhuka Bijumiro-jumiro, the two travelers. When I met them, I was awestruck when they revealed that the Sserulanda Spiritual Center was located in the bush of the poorest district in Uganda, and that they practiced vegetarianism and aspects of the Science of the Soul, a spiritual path into which I had been initiated by Sri Soami Divyanand. So, I introduced them to my associates and friends at Daya Associates - Nu Age Center of Harlem, and we all got very excited. Subsequently, with the help of Bhuka and Noella, we organized a group of eighty-five seekers to travel to the spiritual center in Uganda in the summer of 1987 to participant in what was cast as a Cosmic World Peace Conference.

Held Hostage in Route to the Cosmic World Peace Conference

We arrived at the airport in Uganda just after July 4th, 1987. It was a period in Uganda following a successful revolution, after twenty-six years of civil war and oppression, fueled by the likes of the infamous Idi Amin. We even learned that the family of the rebel leader and current president of Uganda, Yoweri Kaguta Musevene, had taken refuge in the Sscrulanda Center during the war. For whatever divine reason, the people of Uganda had had to endure that DIS-EASE. Our goal was to nourish ourselves spiritually and culturally, and to help in the building of a spiritual city that native Ugandans there saw as a key in the resurrection and healing of, not just the nation, but the planet. (They believed that "Yunganda," its spiritual name, was the nation destined to join together all the nations of the world.)

Of course, people thought we were crazy, especially after we (adults, children, the elderly, and infirm), were held hostage at gunpoint at Uganda's Entebbe airport for four days upon arriving there. Evidently, through a mishap with our hosts, we had failed to secure proper visas. Still, as several of us were politically-militant veterans of the black consciousness movement, we refused their military order to leave the country; after all, for many of us this was a dream come true, a chance to set our feet, for the first time, on the sacred soil of Mother Africa.

Eventually, however, with help from an intervention by the U.S. ambassador to Uganda, we were permitted to enter the country. A caravan of vans picked us up at the airport to drive us to the spiritual center. Along the way, there were human skulls stacked at many crossroads, and several military check points where we had to stop and be questioned. Finally, upon arriving at the village where we were to stay, an outburst of drums, dancing, and jubilation by the people of the village greeted us as we stepped onto that African soil—a dream come true. **The trouble we had gone through had made us appreciate the trip even more. For me, it reinforced a drive inside me that was intent to get to the roots of my existence, not just as an African-American, but as a spirit in search of liberation.**

In returning to the United States, a group of us, led by Ms. Daya Quander and me, incorporated a U.S.A. branch of the Ugandan foundation in an effort to support the building of the spiritual city. Bambi Baaba, by His own admission, was an enigmatic leader. Suffice it to say that in living and traveling with him for a period of time, I learned a lot about the need to "bruise the head of the serpent," that is, to lay the big ego on the ground to be tread upon by the dust of the road, so that the spirit can assume its rightful place (a process which Bhuka, one of his prime disciples, called "Soul-Over-Mind").

Assume the Mood of the Wish Fulfilled

I returned to Uganda in 1988 with my wife Sydnade and children Kemikaa and Kopavi, but not before sweating out how to get there. By this time, I was still operating my holistic practice with intermittent consulting or directing jobs with area community organizations. Bambi Baaba had invited us to return to another spiritual conference there (He actually had never wanted us to leave Uganda after the first conference). But I had no idea of how to afford it as I was about $1,500 short. Still, I made plane reservations anyway, having made up my mind that we would get there by hook or by crook. In those pre-9/11 days you could reserve tickets before paying. Lo and behold, a few weeks before having to pay for the tickets, I opened my mailbox and there sat a check for $1,500, donated by none other than Noella, the same soul who had introduced me to Sserulanda. She thoroughly knew of my work and service and thought I needed to be there.

For me it was a good lesson: **don't let DIS-EASE get you down.** Sadly, however, it was following that trip to Uganda that my first wife Sydnade and I separated and eventually divorced. No doubt, in hindsight, there are many things I would do differently for the part I played in it. However, I am eternally grateful for the support she gave me on my spiritual quest, which took a lot of courage and sacrifice on her part.

Parliament of the World Religions

In 1993, after Sydnade and I separated, but a year before our divorce, she was kind enough to check up on me when I landed in a hospital in Chicago after returning from another trip to Uganda. I had contracted malaria upon returning to the USA to attend a conference—the second centennial Parliament of the World's Religions. It was attended by over 5,000 representatives of just about every known religion and spiritual path on the planet.

Ironically, it was spiritual master Soami Divyanand, who had told me about the conference when I visited Him in his satellite Germany spiritual center in 1992, following the death of my mother. While there, He had given his blessing for my participation in the project in Africa, cautioning me to just remember in my meditations who had originally initiated me. So, in returning to Uganda in 1993, I told Bambi Baaba about the Parliament taking place in Chicago. He slyly looked at me and instructed one of his aides to go fetch something. The boy came back with an original copy of the book published by the first Parliament in 1893!

Following that, I returned to the USA and worked feverishly with my brothers and sisters in the Sserulanda NY office, who were supporting the spiritual center in Uganda, to prepare the way for Bambi Baaba to attend the conference as a dignitary. On the first day of the event, I introduced Him to Soami Divyanand, hoping for some kind of international collaboration and networking (although, as destiny would have it, they were to never be in contact again). Later that evening, I woke up in the hospital. I had feinted, having exhausted myself and come down with malaria in preparing for the conference.

The Healing Power of Water and Rest

In coming down with malaria, the seed had been sown in

Uganda, where, ironically, I had been successfully treating native Ugandans with homeopathy for the condition. It was a valuable lesson. There are always viruses, bacteria, all kinds of pathogens and constitutional weaknesses latent within us, only to be let loose when our resistance is lowered due to some aspect of stress, or enervating lifestyle and diet. **However uncomfortable it may be, I had learned that with proper care, malaria served a great purpose in completely cleaning and detoxifying the body, as long as it was managed properly.** I verified this in my hospital stay in Chicago.

I wound up staying in the hospital for two weeks. Upon entering, they told me I would have to undergo dialysis or risk dying. However, I refused. I knew better, because of my knowledge of holistic health, and I was not intimidated by their veiled threat that I could die—as if my existence would end forever. By then, although I wasn't courting death, I was confident in my recovery and realized that, no matter what, my spirit would live on for eternity.

I also refused any medicine after a quick initial dose of quinine, and only drank water and peed. Neither did I have with me any of my herbs or supplements that normally I would use to help heal myself. Still, after a week, the doctors were amazed at my rapid recovery and were so impressed that they invited me to give two lectures on holistic health to the doctors and interns. (I treated that as a *quid pro quo* to offset the hospital bill I received in the mail weeks later.)

The doctors wanted me to stay longer than two weeks to study me, as I suppose they had had little or no experience with malaria. But I declined, anxious to get back to follow up the Parliament. I realized, too, that spending those two weeks in the hospital was the first "vacation" or prolonged, profound rest that I'd had in over twenty years, as even my travels were work related. So, it was a chance to rejuvenate. Upon leaving the hospital, I found that my eyes were crystal clear, my skin was as smooth and clear as a baby's ass, and when I had to defecate, it went "bloop", didn't smell, and needed no toilet paper to wipe up. (Needless to say, upon returning to a normal diet and regimen, as holistic and invigorating though it was, things weren't quite as pristine clear anymore.) **Of course, it had helped that my basic holistic lifestyle and diet made it possible for me to avoid undue suppressive medical intervention—the kind that one might have to endure when one's condition has progressed to advanced stages before getting treatment.**

The End of an "Internship"

Following the 1993 Parliament, I continued to work and travel with Sserulanda, living alternately in Harlem, upstate NY, Los Angeles, and Virginia. Previously, in the late 1980s, I had lived with Bambi Baaba and a Sserulanda delegation in Belgium for a year. We were seeking funds and investments to build a spiritual city in Uganda. Ironically, when I had returned to the US from Brussels, Belgium, a dear friend who had high security clearance in Washington, D.C. informed me that Sserulanda was a "blip on the screen" of the CIA. After all, how could a rag-tag delegation from Uganda East Africa (which at times included Ugandan government officials) possibly be doing anything other than trying to perpetuate a scam? We weren't, but we did wind up leaving Belgium empty-handed.

After leaving Belgium, attending the Parliament and living with a Sserulanda delegation alternately in Los Angeles for a year in 1994, then in a house in the Bronx, NY, a trailer in upstate NY, and then back in a brownstone building in Harlem in 1995, I eventually wound up living with the group in Fairfax, Virginia in 1996. (I spent a lot of time sleeping on floors and in sleeping bags during my travels with Sserulanda, including in Los Angeles where I was awakened by the great earthquake of 1994.)

By New Year's Day, 1997, after ten years working and traveling with the group, I parted with them, my internship in Sserulanda having come to an end. With the help of soon-to-be wife, Niiva, I packed up and returned to New York to live. It was a mutually arrived at decision by Sserulanda and me. I had begun to increasingly question the pace of Sserulanda's development, the way we were doing business, my inability to meet my basic material needs and adequately support my first two children, and the fact that I wasn't feeling spiritually fulfilled.

Let me hasten to add that no one ever had a gun at my head forcing me to associate with Sserulanda or any of the spiritual guardians I have sat at the feet of. In retrospect, although my allure with Sserulanda might have been tinged with some ego. it was easy for me to believe that, 1) the spiritual center there—near the shores of Lake Victoria in the heart of Mother Africa—was a vortex or cosmic focal point, and 2) our pioneering attempt to build an ecologically friendly spiritual city—Sseesamirembe ("City of Peace")—was a noble effort that would help hasten a purification of the planet.

How many people in this world dare to commit their lives to such an uplifting ideal? I have nothing but respect for the brothers and sisters who are still there toiling to fulfill the vision, even after the passing of Bambi Baaba, During my time traveling, working, and living with the clan of Sserulanda, I did have some life-changing experiences, and learned some invaluable spiritual lessons, some of which were the value of:

1. **The axiom, "To thine own self be true." That is, trust the burning urge and desire within you to grow spiritually and to connect inside with the divine.** Also, realize that whatever teachers, preachers or spiritual masters you attract and decide to engage are part of your ongoing life and spiritual journey. It is commonly taught in the Science of the Soul that while it is difficult on the surface to judge who is or is not a true master, unless you are yourself one, there are some common characteristics to look for. They should:

   a. earn their own living; and not charge money for teaching spirituality;
   b. not discriminate against any human being;
   c. be the embodiment of ethical living, truth and love that should radiate from them, even if sometimes they have to chastise you;
   d. teach the science of how to go inside and become self-mastered;
   e. not profess to be here to start a new religion, but

should teach and demonstrate the ageless wisdom and universal truths and principles underlying all the creation;

f. practice and promote "ahimsa" or non-violence, including refraining from the slaughter of animals to feed our appetite,

g. advocate and practice abstinence from the ill effects of drugs and other opiates and intoxicants;

h. above all, afford an experience with them that should intensify, not diminish, your thirst to know and live the truth and the divinity.

2. **"Seeing is believing."** Admittedly, the spiritual path and experiences with spiritual guides can be an enigma, difficult to understand on the level of the intellect and senses. It requires you to be brave enough to look within, trust and stay focused on that spark within you that has led you to (or from) particular spiritual guides and experiences in your quest to know God. And rather than try to judge them or bemoan the ups and downs you experience in those "internships," be accountable and take responsibility for your decisions, which includes meeting your worldly responsibilities, as opposed to blaming others when you neglect to; and

3. **The value of being in loving community with a group of souls striving to know God, selflessly serving, and pooling resources in support of one another** (even though sometimes there's a lot of DIS-EASE or "rubbing and scrubbing" among you in the process of your purification, which amounts to enduring a "cosmic colonic irrigation". Sadly, a true sense of community is missing in many parts of the world, especially in big cities where many people neither know the tenants in the buildings in which they live, nor the people next door or in the neighborhood.

Out from Under the Radar

In 1997, after leaving Sserulanda, I was burnt out and broke, with two children to support by a previous marriage. I was also tired of working under the radar to avoid taxes, without health insurance, job security, or benefits. In 1998, Niiva and I got married and started to build a life together.

Also, in 1998, spiritual master Soami Divyanand, upon my request, lovingly invited me to work more directly with His mission. I asked for a *Seva*—a way to give selfless service. So, at His behest, I helped incorporate A Centre for the World Religions, the New York branch of an international interfaith organization stressing tolerance and cooperation among diverse faiths. At the direction of Soami Divyanand, and with the help of Ms. Gerlinder Gloekner, and John-Phillip Parkman, I took the lead in negotiating its non-governmental organization (NGO) status at the United Nations where Ms. Anke Kreutzer and I served as U.N. representatives organizing peace forums and meditations. There, we stressed that **one had to neither missionize, convert others, nor leave their chosen religion to come together with others of different faiths.** Instead, why not delve more deeply into one's chosen scriptures and spiritual teachings, seek first-hand experience via meditation, and compare notes? Surely this would mitigate some of the religious conflicts and intolerance infecting the world today.

We, under the direction of Soami Divyanand, submitted a comprehensive proposal to the United Nations to decentralize the UN while preserving the sovereignty of member nations. Our proposal would hopefully limit local and international conflicts and wars, and drastically reduce arms. Thereby, it would divert funds towards sustainable development and eliminating poverty. At the core of our proposal was cultivating world peace, one person at a time, starting with UN civil society and delegates from member nations. Sadly, however, Soami Divyanand who spearheaded this initiative, died before it could gain any further footing.

If You Don't Work, You Don't Eat

My experiences with Sserulanda, Divyanand Foundation, various spiritual teachers and the teachings of the Science of the Soul had a profound impact on the development of the theory and practice of Soul Therapy, which I had employed only marginally while off and on the road for ten years. However, after leaving Sserulanda, I had a more immediate need to figure out how to earn a living. So, I began working two and three part-time jobs at a time and doing my holistic practice on the side while getting up to speed on the rapidly developing "information highway" of the Internet and computers.

One day in 1998, the temporary agency that employed me sent me to work for a few days at Pace University in New York City. At first, I was a temporary employee licking envelopes, filing, and answering telephones on par with the student aides. Nonetheless, I decided that I would be the best envelope licker in the world. On my first day on the job, the executive director said, "I don't know who you are, but I'm going to find a way to hire you full time." She eventually did, after my temp work time at Pace was extended. Subsequently, they steadily promoted me, and I eventually became a Student Success Administrator.

Beyond Intellect—Bouncing out of the Bubble

In the years following 2001, while working at Pace, I was to take a few trips to Soami Divyanand's ashrams in Germany and India. In my time spent there, as had been the case at the spiritual center in Uganda, I had witnessed that some of the poorest, simplest, most uneducated souls are the most highly developed spiritually. I remember one woman who served our delegation unceasingly, like a saint, while we were in Uganda in 1987. I had asked her, "Wouldn't you like to see more of the world and travel to places like the United States?" She answered, "Why? I travel every night." Her journeys were evidently of a spiritual nature, born of her meditation practice and selfless service.

Many spiritual teachers affirm that the simple, earnest seekers on the path are often the quickest to develop spiri-

tually ("The meek shall inherit the earth"). They stress that spirituality can be "caught, not bought" nor can it be gained by intellect alone.

Although, in my travels, I have met many highly intellectual, avant-garde practitioners in several sectors of society, including in the halls of universities, I have found that there's a tendency sometimes for very successful, even progressive souls in diverse sectors of society to narrow their focus to their particular silo. Many, while doing good work, are for one reason or another somewhat suspended in their own bubble. They are not always aware of the equally dynamic work, often directly related to their own, being pioneered by thinkers, planners, and doers in other parts of the world.

> **Although, in my travels, I have met many highly intellectual, avant-garde practitioners in several sectors of society, including in the halls of universities, I have found that there's a tendency sometimes for very successful, even progressive souls in diverse sectors of society to narrow their focus to their particular silo.**

This is true even in some spiritual centers where some of the more highly-developed devotees often say that disciples can sometimes be the most terrible of people as they go through their purification. Spiritual guardians generally teach that the human being's ego-driven intelligence is their worst enemy, and that it is the dominance of the ego/mind over the spirit which is at the root of humanity's problems.

It was working at Pace University that led me to meet a group of world-class intellectuals who not only incorporated metaphysics as a prime aspect of their work but were reaching out to connect with other like-minded people around the world.

The Brazilian Connection

One day in 2009, while sitting at my desk at Pace, I was personally contacted by a group of psychotherapists from Brazil whose writings had already had a profound influence on the therapeutic technique I was developing as a Soul Therapist. I had received a call from Brazil and wondered who it could possibly be. It turned out to be Dr. Claudia Pacheco. She has been one of the heads of a Brazilian initiative, the International Society of Analytical Trilogy, founded by a brilliant Brazilian social scientist and psychothcrapist, Dr. Norberto Keppe. They had evidently discovered my Internet writings describing how I had incorporated their therapeutic technique into my practice. This inspired Dr. Pacheco to invite me to present at their international conference in Saõ Paulo, Brazil in May 2010. I didn't know at the time how I could afford to get there. But she insisted and offered to provide free room and board.

So, I approached Dr. Shakespeare, my manager at Pace, and suggested that, since our division included international programs, why not send me to Brazil to reach out to area universities for potential study abroad or exchange relationships? She said it was a good idea, but it was not in the budget. However, I revealed that I had the room and board covered. "In that case," she said, "we will provide you travel money." So, I accepted the invitation to go to Saõ Paulo to present a paper and speak, and thus began what has become a mutually beneficial and enduring relationship.

My experience in Brazil, where their "healing-through-consciousness" methodology incorporates philosophy, science, and metaphysics, has further emphasized for me the truth that **intellect alone does not confer lasting peace of mind nor ethical action.** I was subsequently invited to present several times at their language school, college, and conferences, and became president of the North American branch of their social activism corporation, STOP the Destruction of the World Association (stopna.org).

While still at Pace University, I finished a bachelor's degree in psychology and journalism. By that time, I was already far advanced in the development of Soul Therapy as a treatment modality. My spiritual experiences and work with Analytical Trilogy had further underscored the importance of incorporating the spiritual element in psychotherapy and other forms of counseling and problem solving. I was not surprised that my introductory psychology course at Pace defined "psychology" as the study of the mind and human behavior, although my study of etymology defined the root *psyche* as "the animating part of one's being—the spirit." **I thus saw that one of my missions was to join in putting the soul back into the practice of psychotherapy and other healing and problem-solving modalities.** I was challenged to do so in 2015 when I was downsized by Pace University.

One Door Closes, Another Opens

At the time, my 14-year-old daughter Amina, from my second marriage with Niiva, cried, "Does this mean we are going to be poor?" (My 17-year-old son Raimi was too cool at the time to outwardly worry, and our 31-year-old daughter Dominique was on her own by that time, as were Kemikaa and Kopavi from my previous marriage). However, my wife Niiva, who worked at Columbia University at the time, didn't blink an eye. She laughed and said, "Now maybe you will write that book you've been procrastinating on and focus on your real work," (referring to Soul Therapy and holistic education). Sometimes, DIS-EASE means that, as one door closes, another opens. So, I decided to rededicate myself to my practice, with her full and loving support.

All of the foregoing experiences, and many others too numerous to mention, are what led me to become a Soul Therapist and Psycho-Spiritual coach and consultant. **I have learned that boldly facing DIS-EASE, going beyond ego and intellect, and appreciating the role of consciousness, universal spirituality and mastership, is often the missing link in more effectively preventing, treating, and persevering in the remediation of ailments, problems, and conflicts in all phases of life and sectors of society.**

I believe that a "DIS-EASE-is-the-Cure" orientation is a unifying element that helps to bridge this gap. It is an approach that incorporates elevating from Mind-Over-Soul to Soul-Over-Mind, as a better way to mind your "business." At the root of this for me has been the search for self-mastery. That is why I wrote this book, hoping that others see or appreciate the wisdom of incorporating this paradigm into their life and work.

PREFACE

Fundamentals of Mind, Spirit and DIS-EASE

In this book, so-called "disease" or "dis-ease" symptoms are seen as the spirit or life force of the organism attempting to heal it, not just in the sense of medical diseases, but what is called here "DIS-EASE" in a broader sense.

In attempting to define "disease" you normally run into a variety of technical definitions that distinguish diseases from disorders, syndromes, and conditions, and these focus mainly on the physical body or body/mind. In any case, one's health is challenged, and equilibrium is upset to one degree or another.

In this book, the challenge to our overall well-being is defined as "DIS-EASE," which includes psycho-socio pathology, and distress or disruption within the life of the organism or entity, whether it be that of the individual, its relationships, an organization, society, or the planet. **As the brother on the block in USA urban areas and neighborhoods would say, "Your ease is dissed," or not respected.**

The psycho-socio dimension of DIS-EASE encompasses the roles of mind (or mindset), consciousness and spirit (the life force), in relation to challenges affecting our well-being. An accurate knowledge of this can determine the degree of suffering and whether maladies or disorders are prevented, properly treated, remedied, or perpetuated. "The mind, in its identity with the ego, cannot, by definition, comprehend reality. If it could, it would instantly dissolve itself upon recognition of its own illusory nature and basis."[3]

In this book, the "Spirit" or "Soul" is used synonymously. It exists as a transcendental energy within and among all human beings, connected to the life-giving root energy (the "ultimate" reality) that permeates the creation, and it embodies the same essential immortal qualities as its Creator. The architect of the universe is whatever created it and you, however you might name it, or not. Surely you can acknowledge that you didn't create yourself, and that there is law, order, and intelligence governing the Creation. Mystics teach that the Creator is not something that can be materially seen by the physical eyes or directly perceived by the bodily mind or senses. Rather, it requires a spiritual experience via access to the higher spiritual realms.

The primacy of a "Soul-Over-Mind" rather than a "Mind-Over-Soul" orientation, in seeing DIS-EASE as the cure, prioritizes cooperating with, rather than suppressing, the life force's systematic effort to maintain or restore the organism's health and well-being, to the extent possible. In this context, **our "business" is much more than money-making, material prosperity, or the exchange of goods and services for profit.** It is anything that you are forced to focus on or get busy with, that causes problems, upsets your equilibrium, has been recurring for a long time, or persistently occupies your mind, often attendant with suffering and anxiety.

You will find this book useful if you and/or people you care about and with whom you are in relationship or with whom you have had to deal, would benefit from:

- Coping better with and recovering more quickly and effectively from the suffering attendant with deaths, break-ups, divorce, job loss, incarceration, public humiliation, or nagging health issues.

- Getting more insight into how to resolve difficult encounters with the opposite sex, family, friends, co-workers, bosses, or workers.

- Seeking or demonstrating a greater sense of freedom and self-expression.

- Boosting self-image and self-esteem.

- Becoming free of things that hold us in bondage.

- Seeing the relationship between challenges faced and what is going on inside the self.

- Getting more insight into the self in relation to how one is seen by others.

- Being better able to take responsibility for the self and make adjustments.

- Rising above the limitations stemming from ways of being raised.

Practitioners of modalities and professional interventions may be better able to help people achieve the aforementioned by adapting a "DIS-EASE is the Cure" orientation, stressing the reversal of "Mind-Over-Soul" to "Soul-Over-Mind" as a "Better Way to Mind Your Business." **It is a paradigm that individuals, organizations, and leaders in business, the social arena, and politics can use to more insightfully and successfully meet life's challenges.** That's what this book is all about. Hopefully, the reader will treat this book and its tenets as a working hypothesis and dare to perform your own experiments, in an effort to fulfill your life or mission purpose.

Normally, the "diseases of civilization" are defined as heart disease, cancer, diabetes, and a list of other ailments, especially afflicting the developed nations of the West. However, DIS-EASE is much more than these physical illnesses. How is it that you can best sustain the health and well-being of organisms in a time of racial, religious, political and xenophobic polarization; economic uncertainty or exploitation; potential nuclear annihilation; terrorism and extremism; religious fundamentalism and fanaticism; wars and conflicts; vacillating, opportunistic, immoral, despotic, or authoritarian leaders; environmental degradation and natural disasters; and extreme poverty or income disparities? And is it not true that this plethora of DIS-EASE is afflicting all of us, irrespective of identity affiliation, fame, wealth, talent, intellect, or privilege?

Higher-Minded, Breakthrough Leadership

This book discusses the theory and practice of what you need to know and do, in addition to and complementary to the conventional teachings and practices of your chosen field of work, or use of professional services, to more effectively deal with the full range of the "DIS-EASES of civilization." That is, if you want to become a more effective, transformational, self-empowered leader and practitioner in your chosen field, in relationships, or even as a family member; and if you yearn to make a breakthrough for yourself, for those with whom you live or work, or for whomever you serve. The intent of this book is to discuss how you and yours can incorporate into your life and work more of a "DIS-EASE-is-the-Cure, Soul-Over-Mind" approach, which leads to more vigorous recovery from:

- the debilitating grip of chronic or recurring conflicts, problems, and ailments; to accelerated solutions, healing, and reconciliation,

- anxiety, suffering, and distress; to increased calm and peace of mind,

- confusion and powerlessness; to sharpened clarity, insight, intuition, wisdom, and a boost to the energy to act and the will to progress spiritually,

- work-life imbalance; to the syncing of career and life purposes, and from

- over-dependence on external or quick fixes with risky side effects; to increased reliance on effective alternative and preventative solutions and remedies.

This applies to you, not only as an individual or partner in a relationship, but also as an owner, manager, or employee in the following classes of organizations or entities: veterans organizations, law enforcement-related organizations, prison institutions, education and youth organizations, human service organizations, religious institutions, large companies, sports teams, small businesses and entrepreneurs, and independent professionals, including athletes and celebrities.

In this book, you will find that a prime cause of DIS-EASE perpetuation is a narrow mindset within individuals, relationships, businesses, and society, estranged from the spiritual or animating part of their being. This all-pervading life force has a direct impact on DIS-EASE and your ability to heal, resolve vexing conflicts and problems or to conduct business. Success is no longer a question of just mind-over-matter or material prosperity and money-making; the challenge in the 21st century is Soul-Over-Mind, for a greater sense of health and well-being, in you and in all persons and sectors of society,

> **a prime cause of DIS-EASE perpetuation is a narrow mindset within individuals, relationships, businesses, and society, estranged from the spiritual or animating part of their being.**

On the other hand, this book is *not* for those who are content to limit their notion of wisdom and "science" to left-brain (linear thinking) or conventional understanding and experimentation, i.e., secular practitioners or narrow-minded "scientists" in the fields of physics, medicine, religion, health, education, or the social sciences. Too many limit their understanding to authoritarian, dogmatic, mind-dominant definitions and practices in their fields of expertise because they lack practical contact with the dimension of life beyond the mind (whatever you choose to call it). This is especially true in the field of the physical sciences.

From Mind-Dominant "Science" to Soul-Dominant "Science"

A simpler definition of *science* includes seeing it as the application of a body of knowledge to produce predictable results. In this sense, the average grandma is a "scientist" in the field of making pancakes. In addition, **there is a "Science of the Soul," a way for you to go beyond the mind and explore or benefit from your spiritual being, in a way that both nourishes your soul and enriches your life on earth.** However, we "cannot enter into higher levels of existence until we advance in consciousness to the point where we overcome duality and are no longer earthbound..." [4]

You can do this just as some of the world's great spiritual giants have done and urged their followers to do. For example, Jesus, Mohammad, Moses, the Buddha, Krishna, Lao Tzu, and a host of other enlightened leaders, philosophers, thinkers, planners and doers, ascended and living. And, as a reminder to Christians, Jesus said, "Verily, verily, I say unto you, he that believeth on me, the works that I do shall he do also; and greater works than these shall he do." (John 14:12, King James Version) **NOTE: according to mystics, the "me" to "believe on" in this quote is not the carnal man Jesus, but His identity as the "Word" or "Holy Spirit" (which is "made flesh" in the form of many different Saviors.

NOTE: Highly evolved mystics and spiritual giants are not limited to those associated with widely-known religions or faiths. It no doubt also includes unsung spiritual and secular giants in the developing parts of the world and a history of oral tradition which is beyond the scope of this book, and much of which has yet to be codified or documented in the writings of the western world. In fact, according to the book *Stolen Legacy*, "The ancient Egyptians had developed a very complex religious system, called the Mysteries, which was also the first system of salvation."[5]

Scriptural or "religious" references, often from the Bible, are cited in this book, not to promote or alienate any particular faith, but to underscore the universality (versus fundamentalism) underlying all religions and spiritual paths. "Loving yourself is loving others, and hurting others is only hurting yourself. If you believe this, then it doesn't make sense that there can be only one religion and that you're going to see God but everyone else is wrong and going to hell."[6]

In fact, excessive fundamentalism is seen here as a primary symptom of DIS-EASE, not only in religion, but in any sector of society wherein one loathes to question their beliefs or open up to examining and testing other points of view. However, any one of you who has tasted of suffering and defied being limited by conventional notions in various fields knows about this. You have probably dared to perform your own experiments based on alternative sources of knowledge and can testify to the results you have achieved. Interestingly, many of the aforementioned spiritual giants were generally unschooled in the conventional sense, but manifested wisdom and mastery in their lives and works equal to or far beyond the best of material-minded scientists in their respective fields.

It is well-known historically that even the great scientist Albert Einstein was one who came around to the belief that "science without religion is lame, religion without science is blind." He is also quoted as saying, "Everyone who is seriously involved in the pursuit of science becomes convinced that a spirit is manifest in the laws of the Universe," and "…the human mind is not capable of grasping the Universe." [7]

Einstein was at least one scientist who recognized that there are regions beyond the mental planes wherein the spirit operates, directly inaccessible to the mind. However, can we not agree that success and accomplishment require you to gain some mastery over your mind? Given that there are at least nine documented forms of "intelligence," maybe we are not as "smart" (nor as unintelligent) as we think we are. Perhaps it is a failure to establish Soul-Over-Mind that places limits on our wisdom, success and well-being.

Who is the Master of our Mind?
Do so-called geniuses and masterminds really have total mastery over their minds? And what separates the enlightened or law-abiding mastermind from the ordinary master criminal, both of whom may suffer from DIS-EASE, irrespective of the intelligence, fame, fortune, or power they wield? For most people, spending just a few minutes trying to meditate proves that the mind has a mind of its own and loves to roam unfettered. This, we posit, is at the root of the DIS-EASE you suffer, irrespective of your ability to concentrate enough to achieve some measure of material success. The fact that you probably find it difficult to stop thinking altogether is a sure sign that you are not in as much control as you may think. In that case, who (or what), then, is in charge and what is its relationship to the DIS-EASE that you suffer?

This book posits that the "DIS-EASE" symptoms you suffer relate directly to the unease of your mind in need of more direction from spirit. This includes not just physical ailments, but also problems, conflicts, and distresses in your personal, family, social, and business relationships and institutions, and in the local, national, and global political arena.

On the other hand, your ability to go within, to "conscientize" or be conscious of hidden, underlying mind/body patterns, is a key to the realization of your highest potential as a human being and the healing of DIS-EASEs, all of which have a psychosomatic dimension—an effect on the body and physical manifestation. Conversely, **you will discover that "inconscientized," suppressed, denied, distorted, or overlooked consciousness of underlying body/mind patterns, aids, abets, and has a causal relationship to recurring or chronic conditions of DIS-EASE.** Just a cursory look at the mentality and behavior of so many of our so-called leaders in the spheres of politics, health, education, and religion, is proof-positive that their mind-based intellect or cunning is having a destructive impact on the world and its people.

Enlightened spiritual beings from time immemorial have taught that your ego/mind is a good servant, but a poor master. "The ubiquitous ego is actually not an 'I' at all; it is merely an 'it'…The irony of human experience is in how fiercely the ego fights to preserve the illusion of being a separate, individual 'I'… the very wellspring of all suffering."[8]

It is your soul or spirit, the animating part of your being, that should be in charge. The spirit is what connects you to your Creator, whereas your ego/mind is all too often vulnerable to the influence of what some religions call "Mammon," or what some label as the negative principality of the creation. Diverse traditions call this principality by different names, i.e., Universal Mind, Lucifer, Devil, Satan, etc.

Whether you believe in some single entity as described in various faith traditions or some Universal power, there are forces operating that tend to limit you, however "successful," smart, talented, or powerful you may be, from being in contact with your life-giving spiritual essence for the healing of personal and societal DIS-EASE conditions. By you establishing the primacy of Soul-Over-Mind via practices that accentuate consciousness, like silent meditation and other forms of going within, it helps to reverse this polarity from Mind-Over-Soul to Soul-Over-Mind, in order to mitigate or remedy whatever DIS-EASEs of civilization that challenges you.

The Challenge of Stilling the Mind and Exploring Inner Space

Many enlightened beings have taught that there is a way of silent meditation that is a key to stilling the mind in order to access Soul-Over-Mind healing. **NOTE: In its truest sense, the highest form of meditation proper is not visualization; it is to "lose the mind," in the sense of rising above the influence of the ego/mind/body, but in fully awakened consciousness.** Silent meditation is a prime method used by saints and enlightened spiritual masters to heal and evolve humankind by teaching them how to contact their divine essence.

NOTE: "Saints" referred to here are not necessarily people who have been canonized by the Catholic church, but are mystics who have reportedly had sublime, first-hand visions and experiences of God, i.e., have revealed God inside; manifested certain abilities related to omnipotence, omniscience, and omnipresence; and act as messengers of the divine. The point here is that, at the very least, they are souls who have mastered meditation at its highest levels. **Because of their omnipresence, true saints are said to be able to communicate with their devotees via what they call** *The Language of the Heart.*

The language of the heart manifests as revelations inside that are not in the form of any particular dialect but are experienced by or revealed to the meditator in their own language. Thus, the advanced or sincere devotee can experience a vision of the saint in their meditation, and they can communicate with one another irrespective of whether the two speak the same language.

It is true that graduating to meditation at its highest levels, like any process worth its salt, takes consistent practice over time; although for the ordinary person, many benefits can accrue along the way. Some may feel that meditating is akin to "doing nothing"—like some sort of escape from one's worldly responsibilities. **However, masters of meditation teach that meditation is meant to be both a source of guidance and intuition in order to act more wisely, and a means by which to experience inner and outer peace, well-being and self-actualization.**

So, although meditation may look like doing nothing, the following story illustrates how one spiritually enlightened mystic refuted this kind of thinking: One day, a saint was sitting and meditating under a tree alongside a road, as he was prone to do each day. A group of laborers on their way to the city for the day's work often chuckled and commented on how it would be nice if the work they had to do could be so easy. Knowing this, one day the Master called out to the laborers and told them he would pay twice what they were getting for their day's work if they would come and meditate with him for a day. So, the next day they happily showed up for work. However, it wasn't long before they stood up and happily ran off to do the day's work, because what they thought was easy, to meditate, was extremely difficult for them.

"That's why meditation can be very hard. It's easy to do nothing, but it is very, very difficult to think nothing. You can never really do that, anyway. The thing is to step back from all those thoughts, like getting out of a rushing river, then just sit there and let the river keep going."[9]

Like in the process of perfecting any task, it may be difficult at first and you may not be able to initially measure the improvement; but if you are consistent and stick to the basics, you will gradually slow down the mind, thus strengthening your meditation "muscle." The fact that it is difficult to control the monkey mind is proof positive that it needs to be corralled. A case in point is the instructor teaching high school students how to meditate. Such youths generally find it very difficult to concentrate for more than a few minutes as the mind tends to wander and they can't keep still. Truthfully, however, every time the teacher intervenes and steers the students' attention back to the process, it is actually enhancing their ability to meditate. This is what gradually slows the mind and leads to higher consciousness. Similarly, every time you return your attention to the object of your meditation, as will be explained later, it gradually results in the slowing down of the mind.

The good news for the ordinary person committed to but not yet skilled in how to silently meditate on a higher level, you can also practice various forms of concentration as a step in that direction—practices that can bear fruit in helping to remedy symptoms of body/mind and social DIS-EASE. More about that is covered later in the book.

Are There Contra-indications for Meditation?

There are those who warn of the dangers of meditation or delving into inner space—the spiritual realms in the beyond. In the same way, many fearfully caution against alternative or other non-conventional approaches to living, especially in the field of medicine. But think about it. What realms are you subject to when you are "possessed" with anger, ego, lust, greed or attachment? Or in extreme cases, addictions of one kind or another that cause you to suffer, however wealthy, talented, intellectual, or high-minded you may be? What causes us to overeat, lie, cheat, steal, get depressed, or smoke cigarettes, drink alcohol to excess, or use illicit drugs (as if trying to get to the bliss and euphoria of heaven "illegally?")

The culprit is not properly practiced silent meditation. In this book, we discuss examples of safe and healthy alternative approaches to interiorization, meditation, spiritual consciousness, and other alternative lifestyle practices. This is based on the teachings or guidance of those who have mastered these sciences, to help you avoid whatever pitfalls you may encounter. As it relates to Soul-Over-Mind, you benefit from exploring the inner spiritual path—not as a substitute for the religion or faith of your choice, or as an escape from the responsibilities of living—but as a way to delve deeper and enrich life in the here and now.

When it comes to difficulties in being able to resolve chronic DIS-EASE or rise above bad habits and behavior, **beware: without spiritually tapping into the spiritual source of wisdom, you may be unwittingly serving or mastered to some extent by devilish-type entities operating through the ego/mind and senses.** This is what makes it more difficult to cure the physical, mental, and social DIS-EASEs of civilization. The good news is, there's a way out, to find relief, which is the subject of this book.

The solution involves nourishing the spirit, mind, and body with the kind of "food" or sustenance that sustains life, i.e., focusing on ways of interiorizing, especially silent meditation, and other lifestyle factors that harness metaphysical energy in the process of establishing Soul-Over-Mind. This ultimately leads you to divine revelations (intuitive spiritual insights); inner peace; divine guidance, wisdom; enhanced energy and vitality; reduced suffering; and accelerated healing of body/mind, relationships, institutions, and society. **You become able to use DIS-EASE as medicine, realizing that DIS-EASE symptoms are spirit's attempt to heal the organism**, whether as an individual, in relationships, or in the organizational or societal context. Soul-Over-Mind can accomplish this.

INTRODUCTION

DIS-EASE in Self, Relationships, and Society

Can we agree that the world as we know it is sick, irrespective of the fame, fortune, or social, economic status of some individuals, institutions, businesses, or nation states? But it's not just what is called the "diseases of civilization," i.e., physical ailments like the number one killers: heart disease, cancer, type 2 diabetes, obesity, hypertension, autoimmune illnesses, osteoporosis, etc. DIS-EASE also includes a host of immune-weakening, stress-related conditions, coping problems, and anti-social, addictive, or psycho-socio, pathological behavior, within self, in relationships, organizations, businesses, and in society and the world.

Factors indicative of the proliferation of the psycho-socio dimension of DIS-EASE in self and society are:

- dysfunctional family, social, or business relationships;

- worrisome money matters, i.e., the cost of education, health care and health insurance, high taxes, unemployment, wages unequal to expenses, not having enough for retirement;

- political strife, wars, crime, terrorism, illegal immigration, racism, police brutality, classism and xenophobic fear of the "other"; and

- environmental pollution, climate change, and natural disasters.

DIS-EASE, in this context, cuts across all levels of economic, class, and political, religious, social or racial status. What all the categories of DIS-EASE have in common is Mind-Over-Soul, alienation from reliance on and contact with the life-giving, healing, spiritual forces within humankind.

Increasingly today, scientists are studying what is called "Psychoneuroimmunology," basically studying the mind-body connection or the connection between psychological processes, the nervous and immune systems, and behavior. For example, looking at psychosomatic conditions or the relationship between the state of mind and emotions relative to physical ailments, conditions, and conditioning. This, however, is only the tip of the iceberg. In order to remedy these conditions, **there is also a trend to move away from over-dependence on quick-fix "silver bullet" solutions and conventional approaches to DIS-EASE treatment, especially the overuse of prescription drugs or opiates to resolve both physical and psychical problems.**

Many are also exploring alternative lifestyles and diets, which includes looking toward inner guidance to cope with and transcend the ongoing pressures of work, school, family relationships, and nagging health issues. This search may include looking more deeply into one's own religion or spiritual beliefs or examining alternatives to conventional forms of religion and spirituality. **You, too, can discover the root causes of DIS-EASE in your life, and resolve whatever may have been blocking you from manifesting the insight and energy to recover. You can increase the will to progress spiritually. You can experience reduced suffering, greater inner peace, more fulfilling personal development, and enhanced family, professional, and social relationships. Soul-Over-Mind can help.**

The Organization as an Entity
Interestingly, many business, money, and wealth coaches

these days stress the importance of living much of one's life through a second type of "person," the corporation, which has many of the rights and privileges of the individual without the same liabilities. However, **organizations also suffer material conditions as they and the populations they service are affected by the contemporary physical, mental and psycho-socio dimensions of DIS-EASE.** They can benefit from incorporating a more Soul-Over-Mind approach in doing business.

What these entities, and the people they employ and serve, have in common is a need to reconcile a dichotomy between personal and collective identity, i.e., alienation, isolation, and individualism versus group consciousness and affiliation. **How do you as an individual survive personally within the collective, or thrive in a world, rampant with psycho-socio pathology that glorifies Mind-Over-Soul?**

Increasingly, you may be among those who are trying to become more conscious of, "Who am I?" that aspect of your being that you have in common with all humanity beyond the myriad "suits of clothing" that your essence wears. But this becomes obscure when you identify more with the body/mind and the material than with the life-giving source of your existence. **Both personal and collective problems share this same pathology: being out of direct touch with a divine connection.** This consists of unwittingly suppressing, denying, distorting, or overlooking—not wanting to see or be conscious of the truth of what is, versus what your mind projects to be. It is this failure that estranges you from fully taking advantage of the spiritual dimension of healing DIS-EASE.

Following are some of the kinds of organizational entities or classes of people in which this plays out, which may be familiar to you. It does so in the form of DIS-EASE or problems and conflicts which would benefit from a more Soul-Over-Mind orientation, to deepen connection to the healing, problem-solving part of being:

VETERANS ORGANIZATIONS that service constituents who suffer from DIS-EASES ranging from Post-Traumatic Stress Disorder (PTSD), disabilities, suicides, drug use, difficult returns to day-to-day, routine family life, family breakups, and difficulties in finding employment;

LAW ENFORCEMENT-RELATED ORGANIZATIONS that must cope with the mental and physical health of police officers who, because of the stressors associated with police work, experience above-average symptoms of the DIS-EASEs of civilization. This includes heart-related diseases, cancer, diabetes, PTSD, obesity, failed marriages, substance abuse, suicide, and in general, distress, anxiety, depression, and relationship issues;

PRISON INSTITUTIONS that manage seriously disturbed inmates with complex, compulsive mental/emotional issues, inmates reacting from having been unfairly incarcerated, and correctional officers who manifest similar stresses and DIS-EASES experienced by other law enforcement personnel.

EDUCATION AND YOUTH ORGANIZATIONS that struggle with the stresses and strains of dealing and communicating with diverse populations of students, often who come from economically disadvantaged communities, and who are affected by a heavy reliance on digital technology and social media. Such institutions face the need to be cognizant of and respectful of multiple forms of intelligence and intuition, as opposed to over-reliance on the intellect and "teaching to the test," standardized tests which allegedly are often culturally biased.

HUMAN SERVICE ORGANIZATIONS that employ workers who suffer severe instances of burnout due to pressure to close heavy caseloads. Many such profession-als overly identify with, or have difficulty dealing with, constituents who suffer from a myriad of social and eco-nomic conditions, including homelessness, domestic vio-lence, substance abuse, and mental illness;

RELIGIOUS INSTITUTIONS, many of whose constitu-ents don't feel completely fulfilled by the congregation's religious rites, rituals and dogmas, or who want a more personal experience of the divine. Many also suffer attri-tion of young worshippers who have increasingly turned toward secularism and away from religious institutions, resisting the idea that conformist religiosity or spirituality is important in their lives. This is part of a larger cultural movement toward materialism and individual freedom, and away from joining large groups or abiding by tradi-tional authorities and mores.

SMALL BUSINESS ENTREPRENEURS AND INDE-PENDENT PROFESSIONALS who suffer the stresses and strains of managing health care, government regu-lations, taxes, uncertainties in the economy, cash flow, overhead expenses, and money management, difficulty generating clients, lack of business training, overwork, ineffective time and resource management, and as a result, some of the typical DIS-EASEs of civilization.

LARGE COMPANIES, including sports teams, that employ and manage workers and face the challenge of enhancing both the well-being, personal growth, and self-empowerment of the worker, as well as corporate profits, social responsibility, community service, and environmental sustainability. Or, the challenge of synchronizing workers' personal fulfillment goals with the company mission. Employees are routinely distressed in striving to maintain work-life balance, improving relationships with management and co-workers, developing better understanding of company policies and communications, and pressing for better training and advancement opportunities, fair wages, and safer overall working conditions.

CELEBRITIES AND INDEPENDENT PROFESSION-ALS, including athletes, who, apart from the impact of external factors, may suffer from several inner issues common to being exposed in the public eye or dealing with the public. These include: drug abuse, addiction, insecurity, self-doubt, depression, fatigue, bad moods, lack of concentration, stomach problems, paranoia, self-hatred, a myriad of stress-related health problems, and the dichotomy of, "Who am I in my core versus my public persona?" This is often especially true of younger, immature professionals, in spite of their material success. Despite being driven in their careers or profession, many still feel a sense of inadequacy, as if they've barely scratched the surface of who they are.

Wherever you may fit in the foregoing classes of people, organizations, and individuals within institutions, you are challenged to effectively address questions of identity, alienation, and individual-versus-group and relationship affiliations, in order to more effectively confront your own or others' distresses and the DIS-EASEs of civilization. And you are faced with doing so in an increasingly globally-conscious world of culturally disparate populations, having to respect diverse ethnicity, gender, race, class, education, age, nationality, sexual orientation, language, and religious or spiritual beliefs.

To meet this challenge, you and other individuals, businesses, and organizations might therefore benefit from more of a Soul-Over-Mind approach, the subject of this book. **How can you employ a more scientific and nuanced understanding and consciousness of a universal, life-giving (spiritual) force in the practical ap-**

plication and methods of resolving the psycho-socio, psychosomatic and metaphysical dimensions of DIS-EASE?

A Soul-Over-Mind Approach to Healing and Problem Resolution

It is the thesis of this book that the answer lies in the "Soul-Over-Mind" approach. This posits that the symptoms of DIS-EASE and problems in individuals, organizations, and society is aggravated by their limitations in consciously identifying with its spiritual dimension. This makes individuals and organizations, by default, vulnerable for rule by the ego/mind, under the influence of universal negative forces. This is seen as the root cause of DIS-EASE symptoms. Enhanced Soul-Over-Mind consciousness is posited as the remedy.

> the symptoms of DIS-EASE and problems in individuals, organizations, and society is aggravated by their limitations in consciously identifying with its spiritual dimension.

Underlying DIS-EASE problems and conditions are suppressed and denied patterns of behavior, emotions, thoughts, and ideas which, 1) aid, abet and have a causal relationship to acute and recurring chronic symptoms, and 2) play out through a universal, four-fold process of creation, from idea to manifestation. However, the good news is that the conditions themselves are designed to bring some consciousness to you, which, if truthfully acknowledged, frees up your spiritual energy to accelerate healing and problem resolution, as an individual, or in relationships, organizations as entities, and society at large.

This book will validate how your cooperation with, rather than suppression of, the symptoms of DIS-EASE, paves the way for Soul-Over-Mind cure, relief, or remission through truth and consciousness.

CHAPTER 1

DIS-EASE is the Cure and DIS-EASE as Medicine

Examines the philosophical and scientific basis of a holistic approach to healing as a template wherein DIS-EASE is seen as the attempt by the spirit or life force to heal the entity of toxemia: mind-body toxins which are seen as the root cause of DIS-EASE.

A more holistic approach to healing is looking at so-called body/mind "diseases" as *DIS-EASE*—an expanded definition of sickness. It is a useful template, the concept of which you can apply to "illness" in your relationships, institutions, and societies as organisms or entities. Hopefully, you, and developmental experts and practitioners in all sectors, are open to employing this template to help remedy common DIS-EASEs that you suffer.

The suffering, pain, and upset of life's conflicts and challenges in individuals and social organisms makes you pay attention to underlying body/mind patterns that you may be denying, distorting, suppressing or overlooking.

The suffering, pain, and upset of life's conflicts and challenges in individuals and social organisms makes you pay attention to underlying body/mind patterns that you may be denying, distorting, suppressing or overlooking. The act of suppression is what has estranged you from the Soul-Over-Mind spiritual energy source of healing or remediation.

Spirit, or what some scientists call "essential energy," manifests in you and each human being as an ongoing heartbeat and breath of life. You are granted an innate awareness—a consciousness—that enables you to act, or not, as a willing instrument or co-creator with this divine life-giving energy. Sadly, however, you have been taught by many in the world of science to believe that your mind/ego, manifesting through the senses and the physical world, is the source of, and ruler over, this essential energy. This mindset influences you to act as if:

- you need not concern yourself with this essential energy or spirit life force because you can't measure it with sense-based instruments,

- it's enough for you to manipulate or fix things using the mind, technology, or drugs and potions of one kind or another,

- you can apply a fix in the social arena by imposing micro-managerial, dogmatic, doctrinaire, authoritarian, imperialistic, or in extreme cases, terroristic control, (which is a form of psycho-socio pathology), and

- it's okay to place undue reliance on drug-like, short-term fixes (or "emergency medicine"), whether in the personal or organizational context, as a prime means of treating DIS-EASE as opposed to research, study, and the long-term application of preventive and curative lifestyle and dietary factors that are in harmony with the essential energy.

To better understand the roots of a Mind-Over-Soul versus a Soul-Over-Mind approach to healing, you can benefit from examining the positivistic and reductionistic model commonly used to treat life's personal and societal ills, a model that you may unwittingly be susceptible to, and which may be a root cause or contributing factor of whatever chronic, recurring difficulties you face.

Positivism and Reductionism - an Imperialistic Approach to Healing

The imperialistic mindset and approach to healing is a signature of largely western world national and political orientation based on the core theories of positivism and reductionism. **Positivism is the theory that theology and metaphysics are imperfect modes of knowledge in comparison to knowledge based on the empirical sciences. Reductionism theorizes that simple physical laws may explain all biological or intrinsic processes.**

It can also be legitimately said that there is a counter school of thinking that deifies religious or psychical ways of behaving at the expense of logic, intellect, and practical materialism. Also, the conventional often ignores traditional or customary ways of being, and the traditional often perpetuates customs and mores that are no longer useful, whereas a Soul-Over-Mind approach is based on "Ageless Wisdom," which transcends time and clime.

In either case, Positivism and reductionism overemphasize verbal, "intellectual," linear or segregative thinking, and negate the validity of intuitive or metaphysical ways of seeing the world. They reduce everything to something you can see, touch, measure, or control (using the mind operating through the senses of perception). **Whatever cannot be understood, or that resists control (like, in some cases, the "other" races, genders, nationalities, religions, etc.), is the enemy to be feared, suppressed, conquered, repressed, or dominated and controlled.** This is a form of hegemony imposed through various forms of authoritarianism, susceptible to both evil-minded and well-meaning (or self-righteous) "left-" or "right-" leaning secular organizations or political orientations, playing out in the form of dysfunction in relationships and organizations, conflicts, corruption, wars, economic exploitation, terrorism, etc.

The War on "disease"

The "war on cancer" is a perfect example of an imperialistic Mind-Over-Soul approach to healing that is being sold to you. After decades of an ongoing search for a miracle cure, the main prescription for prevention or inclusion in treatment, even when drugs and surgery can't be avoided, is what holistic healing practitioners have recommended all along: more whole, natural foods, exercise, and stress-reducing ways of living and interacting.

Another example of the imperialistic approach is a current movement toward using epigenetics to alter gene activity, as if changing the genes without changing the mindset will produce a "cure" of DIS-EASE or aberrant behavior. For some, alteration of genes becomes another effort, like drugs, to effect quick fixes and miracle cures without regard to addressing inherent mindsets, lifestyles, and diets and the derangement of the life force that is trying to heal your organism.

A third example of the imperialistic approach to healing is the germ theory championed by Dr. Louis Pasteur (1822 -1895). It posits that diseases are caused by germs and viruses, whereas other **proponents of a more holistic approach say that germs are present in and feast on decayed and enervated conditions in the host organism.** "Germs and other so-called causes may be discovered in the course of pathological development, but they are accidental, coincidental, or at most, auxiliary."[10] The germ becomes the enemy to be repressed, rather than being agents in your organism's attempt to heal itself.

The germ theory of disease, and the tendency to view drugs and surgery as a first rather than a last resort, is part and parcel of a mind-dominant, left-side-of-the-brain-oriented approach to reality. It is the approach that speaks of "beating the disease," instead of realizing that the DIS-EASE is the cure and should be managed in such a way as to cooperate with what the life force in the organism is trying to do.

A true Soul-Over-Mind understanding realizes that there is a causal world beyond the senses and the mind that can be accessed to bring about and understand effects in the ma-

4

terial world. And there is a science and technology of how to do this. As later covered in this book, you must ultimately "lose your mind" to be successful. That is, you need understand that beyond the finite, temporal, mortal level of being is an infinite, eternal, immortal realm of being that we, as human beings and "the Crowns of Creation,"[11] can have access to. And the spiritual or essential energy manifesting from these realms is the ultimate source of both preventing and healing DIS-EASE.

It is not the contention of this book that you should ignore conventional methods of individual or societal healing and re-mediation. We should just put them in their proper place and see holistic alternatives as complementary, and in some cases, the preferred method, at least as a long-term remedy. Nor is it our contention that a more holistic approach to healing began in or is limited to the West. In fact, traditional healing practices in the so-called "East," in ancient Egypt and prior indigenous cultures all around the globe, are a matter of record. In time, hopefully the work of those who have and are researching the treatment, pre-vention, and etiology of disease in non-Western societies will get the attention and recognition it deserves. This chapter, however, focuses on the roots of DIS-EASE as historically articulated by three great pioneers: Dr. John H. Tilden, with toxemia as a root causal factor in disease; Samuel Hahnemann, who pioneered the science of homeopathy based on the concept, "Like Cures Like;" and Hippocrates who declared that, "Food is your best medicine."

The Roots of Disease in Toxemia

Dr. John H. Tilden was an MD in the USA who lived from 1851-1940 and pioneered an approach to healing citing toxemia as the root cause of Disease. In his landmark book, "Toxemia Explained," he gave a basic definition of toxemia:

> "In the process of tissue building—metabolism—there is cell building—anabolism—and cell destruction—catab-olism. The broken-down tissue is toxic and in health—when nerve energy is normal—it is eliminated from the

blood as fast as evolved. When nerve energy is dissipated from any cause—physical or mental excitement or bad habits—the body becomes enervated, when enervated, elimination is checked, causing a retention of toxin in the blood or Toxemia. **This accumulation of toxin when once established will continue until nerve energy is restored by removing the causes. So-called disease is nature's effort at eliminating the toxin from the blood. All so-called diseases are crises of Toxemia."**[12]

Simply said, all DIS-EASEs, from beginning to end, are effects and cannot be really "cured" without understanding the cause. For you to just treat or suppress the symptoms is not a cure. And when you do recover, it simply means that the "disease" has run its course but can reappear if the root causes are not addressed.

Tilden said that "disease" is really a toxemic crisis, and when the toxins are eliminated below the toleration point, the sickness passes and automatically health returns. However, if the cause of toxic buildup continues, the "disease" symptoms reappear. He taught that what creates toxins and blocks their elimination is what he called "enervation," a stressful way of living caused by lifestyle and diet. NOTE: The emphasis here is on what human beings do to bring on or exacerbate "disease," especially the so-called "diseases of civilization,' apart from genetic or environmental factors over which you may have limited control.

> **Tilden said that "disease" is really a toxemic crisis, and when the toxins are eliminated below the toleration point, the sickness passes and automatically health returns.**

Tilden specifically points to the human being's ways of living and behaving which is indicative of a stressed body and

mind with a direct impact on enervation and subsequent diseases. Instead of human beings mastering themselves (and their minds), they are mastered by their mental and emotional behavior as well as sensual appetites and pleasures. Whether individuals, relationships, organizations as entities, or society at large, mankind suffers from egotism, selfish ambition, envy, jealousy, gossip, and lying.[13] Enervation, and thus toxemia, are further perpetuated by excessive use of drugs and stimulants like alcohol, tobacco, coffee; overeating or improper diets; overwork or dissatisfied work.

All the aforementioned are symptomatic of DIS-EASE in the body, relationships, organizations and society. They are perfect examples of Mind-Over-Soul fueling unwholesome, enervating living. From a Soul-Over-Mind perspective, symptoms of DIS-EASE, far from being the root problem, are the organism's inner attempt to eliminate blocked toxic matter and constitute the spirit's or life force's attempt to heal the organism. What is needed, and what this book is sharing, is how to cooperate with what the organism is trying to do, rather than to merely suppress the symptoms as if that is cure.

A Holistic Approach to Healing

When the organism is overwhelmed and blocked in its efforts to routinely eliminate toxins and you fail to properly nourish it or tune into its innermost needs, it acts on its own to regain homeostasis. It leads to an abnormal or heightened effort to detoxify, which you experience as the symptoms of DIS-EASE. The attendant symptoms of pain and upset make you pay attention to what you otherwise may have been too deaf, dumb and blind to acknowledge. Ideally, the most curative intervention is that which assists your body in this effort to heal itself, as quickly and as efficiently as possible.

Whether the "organism" is a human being or an organization, the root energy to heal it from conditions of "DIS-EASE" is found within it. This energy or life force is always working to evolve and grow the organism, and it does so with much less dis-

7

comfort when you identify and cooperate with it. This becomes even more critical when your organism is already weakened to a certain degree by hereditary and/or environmental factors.

Given the "hand you are dealt," (as in a playing card game) you can still strive to function at the healthiest degree possible under the circumstances. You do this by consciously applying your will to discern what the organism needs and adopting a diet, lifestyle, and environment that, to the extent possible, nourishes and supports the organism. But **unless you realize that the ultimate source of this nourishment is not physical or mental but spiritual, and unless you adapt a Soul-Over-Mind orientation, the "cure" to chronic physical and social DIS-EASE will continue to elude you and keep you and the world on a never-ending cycle of DIS-EASE.**

Homeopathy - Extracting the Spiritual Essence - Like Cures Like

Preceding Tilden, one great human being who discovered a way to tap into the life force that enables the organism to heal itself was Dr. Samuel Hahnemann. He lived from 1755-1843 and pioneered the science of homeopathy, another template that can be referenced to employ Soul-Over-Mind remediation of DIS-EASE. It is called the medicine of "like cures like." It takes substances that might harm you in gross dosages, but be remedial when prepared in micro-doses, if symptoms caused by the gross substance mirror the symptoms exhibited by the patient.

When homeopathic medicines are examined under a microscope, there is no sign of any gross matter, as the original substance has been continually diluted and shaken (dynamized) until no gross matter is left. The theory is that doing so captures the spiritual essence of the medicine which affects the healing.

In a way, this dynamic of "Like-Cures-Like" is similar to the notion that the DIS-EASE is the cure. It is also a precursor to the use of grosser substances in contemporary vaccines; which, however, may not only trigger the body's immunity, but also lead to toxic side effects. However, in homeopathy, unlike vaccines, the patient is not generally in danger of side effects or protracting the disease the substance of which is in the vaccine.

Like the theory of toxemia, homeopathy considers the totality of your symptoms: physical, emotional, mental, and spiritual. In fact, **homeopaths have experienced patients beginning to cure in the process of the homeopath taking the case.** The act of the patient consciously recounting the totality of symptoms and then engaging in a dialectic in answer to the homeopath's questions seems to ignite the curative process. "This individualizing *examination* of a disease case … demands nothing of the medical-art practitioner except freedom from bias and health senses, attention while observing and fidelity in recording the image of the disease."[14]

As will be later posited in this book, in describing the psychotherapeutic techniques of Analytical Trilogy and Soul Therapy, **consciousness is our direct connection to our spiritual life-giving essence which is the source of healing.** And consciousness is beyond mind; this is the beginning of a Soul-Over-Mind approach.

In homeopathy, there is no attempt to suppress the symptoms. Rather, the symptoms are the organism's effort to heal itself. A contemporary of Dr. Hahnemann, and himself a renowned homeopath, was Dr. Constantine J. Hering (1800 -1880). He elucidated what happens when you stop suppressing the symptoms and begin to cooperate with the organism's effort to heal itself using homeopathic medicines (and other holistic modalities). He taught that non-suppressive treatments like homeopathy can lead to what he called a temporary "Aggravation of Symptoms."

Aggravation of Symptoms

In the process of holistic remediation of DIS-EASE, the organism may temporarily revisit symptoms which were suppressed in route to increasingly more chronic conditions. However, this resurfacing can be a sign of cure because of the direction and character of the symptoms, as epitomized in homeopathic modalities of healing. According to Hering's Law of Cure, "The cure is from above downwards, from within outwards, from major organs to minor organs, and symptoms will disappear in reverse order to their appearance, i.e. the first symptoms to appear will be the last to go."

NOTE: *This reinforces the idea that both cause and remediation of DIS-EASE symptoms begins in your mind—that is, a mind estranged from contact with the spirit. Or, in the case of organizations as organism, it highlights how unconscientious policies, procedures, and actions from the top down have a causal relationship to its DIS-EASE or problems; and how conflicts, if addressed rather than swept under the rug, are just symptoms, that, if exposed (an act of consciousness) can lead to solutions. In societies, the idea that change is ignited from the bottom up is another aspect of the idea that "the DIS-EASE" is the cure, if the light of consciousness (spirit) is shone upon it.*

Normally, as "cure" proceeds and some symptoms recur, it is important for you to let nature take its course and continue whatever holistic, curative measures you have employed. Unfortunately, many a person who is treated conventionally or holistically is not told that there may be a temporary aggravation of symptoms in the process of cure or remission. You can recognize curative aggravation of symptoms by noticing that recurring symptoms are less frequent, less intense, of shorter duration, and commensurate with an overall increased vitality.

The patient who is not aware of these phenomena sometimes acts like the drunk or addict who is going through temporary symptoms of withdrawal: he/she opts for the "quick fix or "silver bullet," i.e., he/she imbibes the very substances which helped cause the DIS-EASE condition in the first place. Why? Because, as **in the case of drunks/addicts, a "shot" of drugs or alcohol temporarily stops the withdrawal symptoms or "hangover," which is essentially part of the organism's attempt to heal itself.** (NOTE: Whether individual, organization, or relationship, there are ways to ease the discomfort of withdrawal without suppressing it, which will be covered later in the book.)

Drugs and alcohol—as well as a whole host of other unnatural diet and lifestyle factors—act as stimulants which enervate or use up your organism's energy while providing little or no real nourishment. Abuse of mind-altering substances is actually an attempt to suppress and deny awareness of what is really manifesting within your sphere of awareness. The attendant pain and upset is designed to "conscientize" you, i.e., make you conscious of what is really going on inside of you, but you may be denying and suppressing. This book posits that in most cases you can better heal long-term by letting nature take its course, or at least by nourishing your body with food that sustains life, which will be discussed later in the book. One famous healer who pioneered this approach was a Greek physician, Hippocrates of Kos (c. 460 - c. 370 BCE), considered by many to be the father of Western medicine.

Hippocrates: "Food is Your Best Medicine"

Hippocrates, who preceded both Tilden and Hahnemann, advocated *food* as the medicine of first resort, saying, "let food be your medicine and let medicine be your food." He taught and practiced that **drugs and/or surgery are most necessary as a last resort or as temporary measures when normal lifestyle factors can not immediately effectuate relief.** Even then, however, the use of suppressive drugs or surgery is not necessarily meant to be primary long-term care in lieu of holistic diets and lifestyles. If anything, the two schools of thought should be complementary.

According to a renowned herbalist, Dr. Edward Shook, "Hippocrates, the Father of Medicine, was an herbalist pure and simple. According to botanical history, only 235 herbs were known on the Island of Cos in Asiatic of Turkey, but with a selected few of these he cured his whole nation and the surrounding nations... What an insult to Hippocrates to put his picture on the diplomas of physicians who sneer at, and condemn as useless, the very herbs he used to cure many thousands."[15]

Long term indiscriminate use of drugs to suppress symptoms, without adequate changes in diet and lifestyle, can evolve a condition from acute to chronic. The accumulated side-effects of suppressive drug use, when inappropriately used as a routine, long-term palliative, instead of being used judiciously in conjunction with a more holistic diet and lifestyle, is to create a new and more chronic condition. You may still live and be temporarily freer from the pain associated with the suppressed condition, but your organism may be in a much weaker state, its functions and systems operating at less than maximum capacity, vulnerable and susceptible to further ill health and degeneration.

An acute example of the notion that the DIS-EASE is the cure is illustrated by Hippocrates's advice regarding treatment of the common cold. He has often been misquoted by those saying, "feed a cold and starve a fever." **What Hippocrates actually said was that if you feed a cold, you will have to starve a fever, because the condition will worsen. Therefore, the cold is the cure: the organism's attempt to heal itself.**

On the other hand, when over the long term, the patient pays attention to and cooperates with the organism's attempt to heal itself, i.e. attends to and provides nourishment for its inner needs, the organism gradually works to cure itself to the extent possible, even if you need to incorporate some judicious use of short term "first aid," surgery or suppressive drugs.

Listen to What the Organism and Symptoms Are Trying
to Tell You

When experiencing the symptoms of DIS-EASE, first try to consciously discern what the organism is trying to do and tell you, even if you must take some short-term suppressive measures. Try to determine the root causes of the problem, in consciousness and in the mindset, in order to map out a long-term treatment which will, 1) gradually erase the toxic effects of short-term suppressive treatment, 2) begin to feed the organism what it needs to facilitate the healing it is trying to effectuate, and 3) lead to long-term cure, remission, or remediation. Later, this book will share ways in which you can do this.

Studying the sciences of Toxemia, Homeopathy, and Food as Medicine, are alternative dynamic ways to have a more in-depth understanding or template of how any organism tries to heal itself through the process of DIS-EASE. **Once we learn to work *with* the organism instead of against it, we lessen the need for intense short-term healing crises and overuse of drug-like treatments and their attendant side-effects.** This begins with being conscious of what the organism is experiencing and trying to do by keenly observing and perceiving the physical, emotional, and mental symptoms, i.e., being more conscious.

Being more conscious of our thoughts, words, and deeds—awareness of which we may be suppressing, denying, distorting, or overlooking—in relation to the conditions of DIS-EASE that we suffer, can ignite the healing process. A popular term that describes how we invite the outcomes in our lives is, "The Law of Attraction." However, what is not so easy to explain is the difference between how our thoughts, words, and deeds attract our reality, and our fate or destiny based on the genes we inherit. A deeper understanding of Soul-Over-Mind can help.

CHAPTER 2

DIS-EASE, the Law of Attraction, and Destiny

Examines how our physical conditions are the out-picturing of the thoughts we harbor in the mind, in the context of age-old concepts of nature versus nurture, in relation to notions of fate, the environment, lifestyle and diet, and their role in attracting or resolving the DIS-EASE conditions we face to achieve the well-being we seek.

Since time immemorial, great spiritual teachers, philosophers, scientists, and the learned in every field of endeavor have worked to teach the secret keys to humanity that would elevate us from whatever DIS-EASE condition we face to a higher level of well-being. They have sought to help seekers overcome whatever their inherited limitations and make progress toward sustainable healing and problem solving. From a Soul-Over-Mind perspective, seekers and practitioners of spiritually-based technologies intuitively look first to the soul for the answers, as spirit is the very source of life in the human being.

If you are more and more like many professionals in today's world, you, too, are seeking to tap more into spirituality to: 1) better take advantage of whatever potential or knowledge and talent you possess; 2) overcome obstacles and barriers faced in self, family, relationships, business, and society; and 3) become more reliant on self and spirit for accountability and responsibility in healing and problem solving. But the question is, where do you start?

Start With the "Hand You Are Dealt"

When striving to elevate from the DIS-EASE conditions that you face today, you are confronted with the fact that some are born with the proverbial silver spoon in their mouth, others in poverty; some with strong constitutions, others with inherent weaknesses; some in palaces, others in ghettoes; some with congenital diseases, others with robust health; some with conscientious parents, others with broken families; and some with prodigious talent early in life, while others struggle to be more than "also-rans."

The story of the great genius musician Mozart versus his teacher Salieri is a simple case in point. In the 1984 movie, *Amadeus*, when confronted with the limitations of his own mediocre talent, Antonio Salieri, Mozart's nemesis, believes God has cheated him, while a vulgar, undeserving brat seems to possess divinely-inspired musical gifts."[16]

Ironically, Mozart's middle name, Amadeus, means "Loved by God." But are not the less fortunate loved by God just as much as those who bathe in talent, fame, and fortune? **And is there yet something else that makes it more difficult to start from where you are, and get the best you can get out of the "hand you are dealt" and whatever potential lying within you?** It's the nagging questions of, "Why am I where I am? How limited is my potential? and, Can I really overcome obstacles that stand in the way of transcendence—not just to gain or maintain fame and fortune, but to realize true inner peace and fulfillment?"

Underlying this conundrum or mystery is the question of fate. Is my life pre-determined, or can I change my destiny? Psychologists, biologists, philosophers, and scientists have been grappling with these questions since the beginning of time and have contemporarily framed it mainly in the debate as to whether it is *nature* or n*urture* that has the most influence.

Nature Versus Nurture

"The nature versus nurture debate involves the extent to which particular aspects of behavior are a product... inherited (i.e., genetic) or acquired (i.e., learned) influences...Nature is what we think of as pre-wiring and is influenced by genetic inheritance and other biological factors. Nurture is generally taken as the influence of external factors after conception, e.g., the product of exposure, life experiences and learning on an individual." [17]

Simply said, Nature involves the genetic and DNA blueprint, while Nurture involves changes in the environment or way of living. Two commonly debated factors tend to muddy the waters in determining exactly how much of "nature" is actually set in stone or subject to change. One is behavioral epigenetics, largely still in its experimental stages. It tries to determine the extent to which changes in the expression of genes or nurturing efforts can alter the behavior of genes and thus behavior without changing the DNA. Quite a heady subject to study. For the average person, it's much simpler. **Given the hand I've been dealt, what can I do to improve my life?** To what extent can I alter the environment I live and work in, and what lifestyle factors can I cultivate to enhance my living?

From a spiritual point of view, it is folly to think that simply manipulating or changing genetic expression (like finding a silver bullet miracle fix for cancer) is the magic potion that will result in sustainable changes in behavior or a lasting cure for the DIS-EASEs of civilization, without making fundamental, conscious changes in our lifestyles. And without having a solid understanding of the root causes governing the hand we are dealt, the effects of genetic manipulation, like suppressive drugs, are likely to be short term with attendant collateral damage or side-effects. Since, from a Nature point of view, we are dealing with the very condition we inherit at the moment of birth, there are those who turn to factors of life before and after death to try and explain the matter.

The Sins of the Father and Karma

While it may be difficult to understand or accept why we are dealt the hand we are dealt, there are various explanations that try to explain it. Religionists often evoke, "the sins of the father are visited upon the son," or, "The Lord works in mysterious ways."

16

The mystic or spiritual master may point to your *karma*—the fruits of seeds you have sown in countless incarnations that determine your current fate or destiny, invoking the aphorism, "As you sow, so shall ye reap," or, "An eye for an eye and a tooth for a tooth" (not suggesting revenge, but in terms of reaping what you sow). Ironically, **although most all believe that "you reap what you sow," what is more difficult to digest is the notion that, "If you are reaping it, you sowed it." If this is true, the question is, when did you sow it?**

The scientist glibly speaks of the law of cause and effect, saying that every action has an equal and opposite reaction, but strive mainly to manipulate physical phenomena, irrespective of root causes. For instance, it is common knowledge in the scientific community that they know more about the effects of gravity and how to manipulate it than the underlying principles of what it is and how it keeps the planets in balance. Still, even without knowing root causes, we wisely march on, hopefully learning how to delve more deeply for answers.

For many, some of these explanations about the apparent inequities of life evoke visions of unequal justice and mercy, or the victimization of those suffering difficult-to-explain struggles. Whatever the case may be, we are all stuck with the "hand we are dealt," the mind/body, genetic and environmental conditions we are born into. The question is, how can we get the most out of it; and **how can we maximize our potential, health, and well-being given where we start?** Many cultures turn to the use of "oracles" to help tap into the spiritual dimension to explain this and guide the way toward more effective living.

Divination and the Use of Oracles

Broadly speaking, an *oracle* is seen as, "…a message from a god, expressed by divine inspiration … In antiquity, 'the agency or medium of a god,' also, 'the place where such divine utterances were given.'"[18] It consists of using certain devices to get divine guidance in addressing the ups and downs of life, and in making important decisions. **One saying passed down states** that, "**the oracle is food for the able-bodied human being to grow spiritually, in the absence of direct, first-hand spiritual experience.**"

To help explain this from a more esoteric point of view, let us break down the word "oracle." 'Ora' refers to the "Word" or Holy Spirit, the root energy that various spiritual and religious traditions refer to as the source of the life force in the creation; its essential qualities are immortality—omnipotence, omniscience and omnipresence—the same qualities as the Creator of all. However, as it applies to the mundane and worldly concerns of human beings, the 'cle' refers to the cycles of time in the creation, subject to mortality. Thus, the oracles purportedly aim to help humans to more effectively use their spiritual energy to navigate in space and time. It's the difference between 'Zero' (0) which represents the immortal All, and the lemniscates (∞) which represent the All manifesting in the perpetual cycles of time.

Some, like the psychotherapist Carl Jung, equated the use of oracles to tapping into the collective unconscious. In any case, there are millions around the world who swear by the use of certain oracles to help in alleviating the DIS-EASEs of everyday life. Some common oracles include Tarot cards, the I Ching, Ife Cowry shells, and astrology. Proponents say that beings of the angelic ranks are the forces that dictate the arrangements of the readings.

For those who would like to explore the oracles, here is one word of warning given by more mature, enlightened, spiritual and scientific-minded practitioners of the oracles, whether it be the aforementioned oracles or even a psychic acting as an oracular medium of sorts: ONE SHOULD NEVER USE THE ORACLES FOR FORTUNE TELLING. If used at all, they should be like a weather report, letting the seeker know the states of energy manifesting that might affect the action or decision that a querent or seeker wills to take. Then see for yourself if it works.

The seeker, coming from a Soul-Over-Mind point of view, strives to go beyond the confines of the material world and pursue more direct spiritual experience via various con-

sciousness-raising and spiritual technologies. However, many users of the oracles insist that it may serve as a sort of map of the conditioning of the soul at the moment of birth or later points in time (i.e., like a coat of paint covering a light bulb). Whatever the antecedent cause of this conditioning, oracles help some seekers to accept, rather than fulminate or begrudge, the hand they are dealt, in order to free up the mind and for the person to progress in spite of apparent pre-conditioning. It's like the people on a sinking boat. One person is cursing and fretting as to, "How in the hell did we get in this fix and who is responsible?" While others are bailing out water, plugging up leaks, casting out life preservers or "radioing" for help. This points out the importance of the state of mind, IN THE MOMENT, in addressing conditions of DIS-EASE, irrespective of the possibility of causes outside the confines of a present lifetime.

The Secret of Mind Science and Positive Thinking

What most religious, spiritual, or psychological philosophies have in common is the notion that whatever the hand you are dealt, **one of the best ways to affect your destiny is, to the extent possible, judiciously monitor and carefully choose your thoughts, words, and deeds. Proponents of positive thinking and mind science teach that thoughts are things that attract or impact the outcomes in your life**. However, from a Soul-Over-Mind perspective, there are other very important factors not always considered in assessing the impact that your mind and intellect is having on wellness or DIS-EASE in your life:

In the words of Kirpal Singh, an acclaimed Saint who once addressed the Ninth General Session of the United Nations UNESCO in 1956, "Allegorically, the present state of the individualized soul is described as riding in the chariot of the body, with dazed intellect as the charioteer, the infatuated mind as the reins, and the senses as the powerful steeds rushing headlong into the field of sense objects and sense pleasures."[19]

It is for this reason that it is so important to **actively strive to engage the spirit in order to tame this bucking bronco called**

the mind, so that you can master it rather than have it master you. When reading and hearing many of the proponents of mindfulness or positive thinking and mind science, it would seem that they are saying, in the words of author Napoleon Hill, "Whatever the mind of man can conceive and believe, it can achieve."[20] This is a major tenet of a wildly popular book entitled, *The Secret*, by Rhonda Byrne, who wrote of what she called "The law of Attraction." However, from the perspective of Soul-Over-Mind, one need be very careful in embracing and employing this teaching.

The Secret Law of Attraction

A plethora of personal transformation specialists, spiritual messengers, money-making experts and professionals and authors in the fields of quantum physics, psychology, metaphysics, coaching, theology, finance, etc., including the famous Oprah Winfrey, are quoted in the book, which also boasts a list of "secret teachers," from the Buddha to inventor Thomas Edison. According to Ms. Byrne, "There isn't a single thing that you cannot do with this knowledge. It doesn't matter who you are or where... The Secret can give you whatever you want...Like Aladdin's Genie." [21]

Spiritual teachers don't deny that it is better to think positively than negatively. However, there are other things to consider in using thoughts to wish for things, as per the law of attraction. This is especially true for those who become frustrated and find that it's not so simple; nor, they say, does it always seem to work, in spite of one's dedicated efforts:

1. **What did the 5-year-old girl who got raped think to attract that attack, and if so, when did she think it?** Did the thinking take place in a previous lifetime? Or was it pre-coded into her genes?

2. **Are there any limiting factors that might, in one's lifetime, preclude the achievement of a thought-goal one thinks up?**

20

Whether you accept the notion of karma or destiny determined by one's genetics, might there be mitigating factors determining whether what you choose to aim for in this life can realistically be achieved?

Note: Enlightened saints say that some seed thoughts may have to wait for future lifetimes to manifest. Or, there may be present karma that must be mitigated in this lifetime that may preclude the achievement of a sought-after goal. And no new thoughts, words, or deeds can erase karma destined to pay in this lifetime; rather, remorseful good deeds will generate their own "good" karma to be realized in this or future lives.

3. **Is it wise to use the law of attraction to primarily amass material things?**
   From a Soul-Over-Mind perspective, this invokes the Biblical saying, "For what shall it profit a man, if he shall gain the whole world, and lose his own soul?" (Mark 8:36 - KJV) …or lose his present health and well-being?

4. **Of the infinite goals one might choose to achieve, is there some font of wisdom that one might employ to choose aims that are most beneficial to one's overall and spiritual development?**
   Is it wise to rely mainly on the ego-mind operating through the senses of perception to determine what one wills to achieve, or does it further one to develop a more Soul-Over-Mind source of intuition in making one's choices?

This is a reminder of the woman who had a perfect visual image of the tall, dark, and handsome man she wanted to attract as a partner. She did, in fact, attract such a man. However, at last report, she was throwing his belongings out of her window and told him, "Don't let the door hit you in the back." The moral of the story? Be careful what you ask for, you might get it. What-

21

ever one may think of the root cause or precedent governing the DIS-EASE conditions one is experiencing, it does further one to be very careful about the thoughts percolating within their sphere of awareness that might have led to or abetted the conditions that mirror those thoughts. The conditions experienced, say advocates of positive thinking, are basically answers to your "prayers," i.e., an out-picturing of the seed thoughts you have sown.

"Prayer - The Art of Believing What is Denied by the Senses"[22]

Neville Goddard, a Barbadian author, wrote a best-selling book entitled, *Resurrection*. In it, he counseled people to take heed of the Biblical verse in Mark 11:24 (English Revised Version), which says, **"What things soever ye desire, when ye pray, believe that ye have received them, and ye shall have them."**

In other words, assuming in the present the mood of the wish fulfilled is what objectifies your desire. Neville urges you to imagine NOW what it would feel like had you already achieved your goal. He says, **"Awaken within you the *feeling* that you are and have that which heretofore you desired to be and possess,"** and it will **magnetically manifest in your life.**[23] He says that the "Sabbath" is the act of resting and allowing manifestation to take place in its own time, like mystics teach us to not be attached to results.

Preferably, assuming that what you will to achieve is in harmony and in tune with the natural and divine laws that are at work, it makes sense to apply this teaching to treating or preventing the DIS-EASEs of civilization that we suffer. In this light, Neville cautions the seeker to also take care of how and what you think about others: **"If your fixed idea is not subjectively accepted by the one toward whom it is directed, it rebounds to you from whom it came**...A person who directs a malicious thought to another will be injured by its rebound if he fails to get subconscious acceptance of the other." [24]

This might, in some cases, explain how the DIS-EASE you suffer is related to the thoughts you transmit, not just to yourself, but to others. This is why it is so important in your relations with self and others to carefully monitor your thoughts, words, and deeds so that you can better see the relationship between them and the DIS-EASE conditions you suffer, in order avoid reaping negative results. "…you are the gardener of your own mind. It's the idea that you have to take responsibility for your thoughts, to catch and stop yourself from thinking thoughts that are inappropriate or hurtful."[25]

One especially harmful habit that feeds DIS-EASE is name-calling or labeling a person, yourself included, as if your or their entire being is synonymous with some bad behavior. In other words, "Hate the sin, not the one who sins." While this is not a license to excuse the sins or sweep knowledge of them under the rug, how we deal with the obstacles inherent in sins is a key to healing and resolution.

Because of the mysteries of why we are dealt the hand we are dealt, and its impact on the goals we affirm in this

it is folly to think that mentalizing alone is enough to heal the mind of its patterns that aid, abet, perpetuate and have a causal relationship to the DIS-EASE that you suffer

lifetime—whether you see it in terms of karma, inexplicable sins of the father, or genetics—it is folly to think that mentalizing alone is enough to heal the mind of its patterns that aid, abet, perpetuate and have a causal relationship to the DIS-EASE that you suffer. As stated in the beginning of this chapter, healing and resolution begins with squarely facing up to the hand you are dealt, the obstacles in front of you. This ensures that you get more "bang for your buck" (than otherwise would be the case) with the positive seed thoughts that you currently sow. Part of the "hand we are dealt" are the socio-political and environmental conditions challenging humankind today.

Results of the Collective Mindset on Planetary Conditions

Based on landmark research in psychoneuroimmunology regarding the effects of human thoughts and emotions on physical health and disease, **it's not hard to imagine the impact of the mass mindset conditioning of human beings on the planet.** Humans are spirits wrapped up in physical bodies that consist basically of water and earth or the fusion of plant life. Some researchers have written about the effects of human thoughts on water and plants.

THE HIDDEN MESSAGES IN WATER

Studies have been done on how "good" thoughts, music, and words turn the crystalline structure of water into beautiful and delicate shapes, but "bad" [thoughts] deteriorate crystal structures. Author and researcher Dr. Masaru Emoto claims that our consciousness has the power to change the quality of water. On the website Amazon.com, an author of the book *Sacred Contracts*, Caroline Myss, writes about how Dr. Masaru Emoto's first book, *The Hidden Message in Water*:

> "told about his discovery that crystals formed in frozen water revealed changes when specific, concentrated thoughts were directed toward them. He also found that water from clear springs and water that has been exposed to loving words showed brilliant, complex and colourful snowflake patters. In contrast, polluted water, or water exposed to negative though formed incomplete, asymmetrical patterns with dull colors. The implications of this research creates a new awareness of how we can positively impact the Earth and our own personal world. This book takes you further and deeper into how you can affect your own personal healing by reading it."[26]

Is it not logical to believe that since about two thirds of both the world and our bodies is made up of water that our individual and collective mindsets, thoughts, and emotions

have an effect on the DIS-EASE suffered by the planet in the form of aberrant behavior, wars and conflicts? This is no less true of the impact of humanity's mindset on the physical conditions of the earth such as earthquakes, hurricanes and all kinds of natural disasters.

THE SECRET LIFE OF PLANTS

The book, *The Secret Life of Plants*, discusses how plants may be sentient, despite their lack of a nervous system and a brain.[27] Many of us have experienced how the health of plants can be affected by the thought, music, etc. that vibrates around them. Again, since both man and his environment are made up of constituents of the plant kingdom, it follows that our thoughts affect the body and planet, in terms of symptoms of DIS-EASE.

While there is yet much research to be done regarding the macro effects of human thoughts and emotions on the individual and the planet, common sense tells us that the law of attraction is not limited to our individual lives, which is where relationship, organizational, social, business, and planetary healing should begin.

In light of the reality of the DIS-EASE conditions on all levels on the planet, it makes sense to reflect on how the symptoms themselves are sending a message to us; they act as vehicles through which the soul energy of the Creation is moving to heal us; if we would only be conscious of it and cooperate rather than suppress, deny, distort, and overlook its roots in our individual and collective mindsets.

> **There are some great books that clearly point out how DIS-EASE symptoms relate directly to certain mindsets, emotions and habitual ways of acting.**

Psychosomatic Correspondences to DIS-ESE Symptoms

There are some great books that clearly point out how DIS-EASE symptoms relate directly to certain mindsets, emotions and habitual ways of acting. Louise Hay, whose book you will find in the bibliography, lays out a literal dictionary of such correspondences. As pointed out earlier, the mindset may serve to aid, abet, and have a causal relationship to the DIS-EASE symptoms. Knowledge of this can help the individual and practitioner to zero in on some of the underlying factors related to the conditions. It could be as simple as:

- **Heart Disease:** Lack of joy; a hardening of the heart
- **Cancer:** Deep seated grief and resentments
- **Diabetes:** Longing and sorrow for the sweetness in life that is missing
- **Arthritis:** Severe criticism of self and others, feeling unloved and resistance to emotion
- **Alzheimer's:** Hopelessness and helplessness, refusing to deal with the world as it is
- **Hypertension:** (high blood pressure) a strong need to be in control of everything
- **Overweight:** Need to feel protected, running from feelings, self-rejection
- **Aids:** feeling defenseless, hopeless, not good enough, nobody cares
- **Skin problems:** dislike of self; insecurity; unresolved feeling of irritation
- **Addictions:** (Alcohol, drugs, etc.) running from self, self-rejection, void in the soul

Sometimes it is as easy as:

- *headaches* = self-criticism
- *eye problems* = refusing to see
- *ear problems* = refusing to hear
- *voice problems* = an "acid tongue" or a need to speak up
- *stiff neck* = refusal to see all sides of issues
- *shoulder problems* = feeling burdened
- *back problems* = feeling unsupported (not recognizing the ultimate source of support in the spirit)

- *respiratory problems* = feeling smothered or needing to get something off your chest
- *urinary tract infection* = pissed off, but suppressing it
- *stomach problems* = need to have the guts to proceed
- *hand problems* = can you handle it?
- *leg problems* = resistance to moving forward
- *knee problems* = stubborn pride and ego, etc.

The foregoing are not hard and fast rules that dictate a cause or remedy. Rather, they are just factors that the practitioner can take into account in diagnosing the DIS-EASE conditions. In modalities such as Chinese medicine, homeopathy and psychosomatic psychotherapy, practitioners look at the relationship between mind, actions, and DIS-EASE symptoms in relation to specific bodily organs, structures, and systems. The advanced practitioners go even beyond this and look at consciousness and the spiritual dimension as a source of the healing energy. Consciousness is what we have in common, irrespective of differences in religious or spiritual orientations, and it is a vital key to the prevention, treatment and healing of DIS-EASE.

The Obstacle is the Way

Consciousness of (not suppressing or preoccupation with) the obstacles we face is one factor in reshaping our environment and mitigating the DIS-EASE we suffer, along with, 1) adapting diets and lifestyle factors that enable us to better tap into spirit and subtle energies that make up the "food" that sustains life, and 2) cultivating mind/body patterns that support healing, health and well-being.

This is another way of saying that the DIS-EASE is the cure. However, to make this work for you requires a Soul-Over-Mind orientation. One of the keys to Soul-Over-Mind is consciousness, being aware of the underlying mind/body patterns we are born with or into, or that may be driving us, moment to moment, day-to-day.

In the next chapter, you will learn of an avant garde form of psychoanalysis called "Analytical Trilogy," that calls this process of awareness, "conscientizing." The key to their success has been integrating metaphysics along with science, philosophy, and a knowledge of the psychosomatic dimension into their psycho-therapeutic approach, to help individuals and organizations heal and successfully alleviate personal and psycho-socio pathology.

CHAPTER 3

DIS-EASE, Analytical Trilogy and Psychosomatic, Psycho-socio Pathology

Focuses on the relationship of the mind to DIS-EASE conditions, including a dialectical approach to psychotherapy that combines philosophy, science, and metaphysics; and the relationship between individual pathology and psycho-socio pathology, and resulting psychosomatic conditions.

Analytical Trilogy (*A.T.*) is a psychotherapeutic science and methodology that examines how truthfulness ("conscientization") is used as an antidote for problem conditions, and how "inconscientization," the suppression of truth and consciousness, leads to psycho-somatic conditions, i.e., those brought on by the emotional, mental state of a person.

Analytical Trilogy is a true Soul-Over-Mind solution for individuals and professionals who are looking for answers to how to deal with DIS-EASE and the inherent trauma, distress, alienation, and identity crises experienced by their clients, themselves, and society at large. As such, it is a way of making a spiritual connection and using trauma as an opportunity to heal by conscientizing all that is happening. In doing so, you may discover the root cause of the trauma and trigger a process of remediation.

The Science of Analytical Trilogy

A.T. goes beyond conventional notions of psychotherapy in incorporating science, metaphysics, and philosophy. It posits that there is more to "science" than the physical, natural world and phenomena. It includes the metaphysical, from a more universal perspective, and considers the philosophical framework underlying personal and psycho-socio pathology.

This psycho-therapeutic methodology has been pioneered by a Brazilian psychoanalyst and independent physics researcher, Norberto Keppe, PhD, who, as of 2019, has authored thirty-nine books on the subject. In 1970, he founded and became president of the Society of Integral Psychoanalysis in Sao Paulo, Brazil that operates a clinic treating patients through Analytical Trilogy.[28] In it, its Vice-president, Dr. Claudia Pacheco, wrote of patients cured of psychosomatic-related illnesses. In her book, *Healing Through Consciousness*, she documents testimonials of patients reporting having been healed of rheumatism, high blood pressure, bronchial asthma, epilepsy, and a host of other ailments.[29] However, one of the greatest challenges facing the Society is to do for the society what it does for the individual.

> **there is more to "science" than the physical, natural world and phenomena. It includes the metaphysical, from a more universal perspective, and considers the philosophical framework underlying personal and psycho-socio pathology.**

The Marriage of Personal and Psycho-socio pathology

Keppe labels this union, "The Psycho-socio pathology of Power." In his book, *Liberation of the People, the Pathology of Power*, he clearly delineates how a solution must both treat individual pathology and also find a way to similarly treat sociopathology. His organization has therefore created what they call "Trilogical" cooperative enterprises, both businesses and residences, that address three main problems:

1. WORKER-OWNER ANTAGONISM: "In Trilogical Enterprises … all the people who work in the company are shareholders … based on the work and effort of the participant in benefit of the organization."[30] (With profit-sharing based on work, not investments)

2. MONEY-MAKING WITHOUT WORK: The Trilogical model eliminates the kind of speculation inherent in venture capital funding and treats capital investments as interest-free loans which are repaid not with interest, but with value accrued through inflation.

3. THE PSYCHOPATHOLOGY OF WORKERS: In Trilogical enterprises, "everyone in the enterprise participates in weekly meetings with peers and colleagues, receiving direct feedback from them,"[31] assisted by trained facilitators. In these meetings, psycho-pathological behaviors of workers that limit productivity are "conscientized," made aware, and not suppressed, which is what normally increases neurotic behavior.

The details of how Trilogical enterprises work is more intricate than can be outlined in this book. However, the founders of the International Society of Analytical Trilogy have created several thriving Trilogical residences and businesses in Brazil. You can get more information at http://www.richjonesvoice.com/transcripts/enterprises.pdf and in Keppe's book, *Liberation of the People, the Pathology of Power*.

Apart from the different approach to money and investment, the critical element in the success of Trilogical Enterprises is the inclusion of metaphysics, philosophy and science in the process of bringing consciousness to the shareholders of how their mind/body pathologies estrange them from the essence of their being, the principles of which follow in this chapter. This approach to psychotherapy, especially in the context of metaphysics, has also been applied to the field of science, especially physics, which resulted in the development of a sustainable, 90% energy efficient motor that has won international awards.

Keppe Motor and the Essential Energy

The work of Dr. Keppe "has inspired engineers Cesar Soos, Alexandre Frascari and Roberto Frascari to produce a motor that captures Essential Energy, a free, primary energy source which is infinite and exists everywhere in the entire universe. The production of the Keppe Motor demonstrates that the union of science with philosophy and theology is finally here." (https://www.cultureunplugged.com/documentary/watch-online/play/13066/Disinverted-Metaphysics---Keppe-Motor-Documentary-Welcome-to-the-Future)

You can read more about this in Keppe's book, *The New Physics Derived from a Disinverted Metaphysics.* As such, Analytical Trilogy is a true example of a Soul-Over-Mind modality geared to prevent, treat, and heal DIS-EASE by reversing a Mind-Over-Soul, "inverted" human state wherein humans are dominated by the mind/body rather than their spiritual nature.

Inversion and the Descent of the Human Being

Dr. Keppe defines this **inversion** as a psychological process … in which values and the perception of reality are inverted in the individual and in society. Examples: seeing good in something evil, and evil in something good; believing that reality, not fantasy, causes suffering; seeing work as a sacrifice and laziness as pleasurable; thinking that love brings suffering and pain; and making wealth, prestige, and power the most important goals of all.[32]

In their Mind-Over-Soul descent from the heavenly realms, humans have come to invertedly identify with the mind/body being supreme rather than the soul essence, and humans thinking that they are the "suit of clothes" that they wear, rather than the spirit that wears it. Dr. Keppe has coined other very insightful terms which amplify our understanding of this inversion:

32

1. **Inconscientization:** The willful attitude of concealing, repressing, or denying one's consciousness. Hiding from oneself something one does not wish to see.[33] Dr. Keppe defines this not seeing as an expanded definition of **"envy,"** i.e., based on the Latin root of the word: "invidere" (in-=non, videre=to see). Keppe sees envy as a psychological blindness, a negation of awareness, an unconscious wish to destroy the goodness and beauty we see, not just in others, but in our own lives as well.[34]

2. **Theomania:** Fighting against life, against reality, and principally against the consciousness of our errors. And the impending danger to which we are subject is the danger of having to cease being the godlike creatures we think we are. Because of this Theomania, we create our own torture chamber. Man struggles against his nature and his health and kills himself, while firmly believing that his interests are directed toward reality.

It is this inverted Mind-Over-Soul orientation of humans, and their inconscientization, envy and Theomania, which invites evil and demons to take possession of the human being's faculties.

Demons and Evil in Everyday Life

To better understand the day-to-day body/mind distress suffered by people, Dr. Keppe has written extensively on the manifestation of psychopathology in the form of demonic possession, which he has chronicled in his book, *Psychotherapy and Exorcism*.

Demonic influence comes in the form of a, "long standing compulsive behavior pattern … an addiction, and an addiction lives inside you as a quasi-entity or subpersonality, an energy field that periodically takes you over completely … if you are identified with the internal voice due to lack of awareness … At other times, the addiction may bypass the thinking mind … trick you into doing what it wants."[35]

Think about it. What forces are people subjected to when "possessed" with anger, ego, lust, greed, or attachment? Or, in extreme cases, addictions of one kind or another? What causes us to overeat, lie, cheat, steal, get depressed or smoke cigarettes, drink alcohol to excess, or use illicit drugs (as if trying to get to the bliss and euphoria of heaven "illegally?) What kind of demonic forces might be at work in the immune-weakening, stress-related conditions, coping problems, and anti-social, addictive, or psycho-socio, pathological behavior, within self, in relationships, in society, and the world? According to psychologist Dr. Edith Fiore, "Possession can help us to understand abnormal behavior, personality, mental, emotional, and physical problems."[36]

Surely, if there are demonic forces at the root of a suffering mankind in everyday life, not just personally in the exorcised-demon-possessed, but the ordinary person, it would help to know how to banish these alienating evil forces. From an *A.T.* point of view, "The idea of being a victim of evil is quite a comfortable one, but in fact, what's really going on is that the human being chooses and even summons his demons, thereby actually selecting the type of evil he wants in his life."[37]

Dr. Keppe says, "I believe that anyone who does not admit that demons exist, or worse, declares that he is not influenced by them, is entirely under their control. In other words, however much demons reject divine energy, they still cannot live entirely deprived of it without suffering terribly."[38]

Like *A.T.,* a Soul-Over-Mind perception sees this rejection of divine energy as an attempt of demonic forces to alienate humans from their true essence and divine calling, to prevent them from realizing their divinity and escaping demonic control. The antidote for this, according to Dr. Keppe and *A.T.,* is the process of **Conscientization.**

Conscientization and Interiorization

To conscientize is a word that Keppe coined in English … to describe the psychological process of becoming aware of reality, both external and internal, through a mixed process of feeling and

34

knowing. In addition, he describes what he calls **Interiorization**, "the comprehensive process of perceiving the existence of an inner psychological universe greater than our external universe: virtually, the existence in us of the beauty, truth, and goodness of the Creator, the most important process in Analytical Trilogy, because it constitutes a return to one's inner self, to the source of life and happiness.[39]

> **To conscientize is a word that Keppe coined in English … to describe the psychological process of becoming aware of reality, both external and internal, through a mixed process of feeling and knowing.**

Interiorization also alerts humans to how what they are experiencing inside relates directly to what they are experiencing outside in life. This often manifests as **projective identification**, wherein one is guilty of the very thing one accuses of others, as if others are the cause of all one's problems; or **Projective Idealization**, in which one's fantasies about themselves are projected onto others rather than seeing the truth within themselves and others.

In the lexicon of Dr. Keppe, truth, goodness, and beauty within self is synonymous with God or being. The practical application of this is reflected in the human's relationship with the Creation which, like humanity, is an offspring or spark of the divinity of God, which, however, must be nourished in a way that sustains life. One does this by truthfulness or conscientizing and doing good, which, so teaches Keppe, is the essence of ethics. He says that this, along with cultivating aesthetics, is a way of tapping into or accepting being (and thus healing).

The Healing Effects of Art and Aesthetics

Keppe teaches that harmony in life comes from art and aesthetics, which he equates with inner equilibrium; it nurtures the emotions as well as the thoughts in a way that nourishes humans' bodies, via their conscious effort to do good in thought, word, and deed. Divine thoughts and emotions sustain the body/mind of self and others, while negative thoughts destroy self and others, including the environment.

In his various lectures and broadcasts, Keppe goes so far as to say that, "It's not possible to have real knowledge of anything (philosophy, politics, theology, economy) if there is no contact with aesthetics," to spread goodness and ethics, as well as truth within our world. However, on a day-to-day basis there are psycho-socio, pathological, and distress factors that limit the human being's ability to appreciate aesthetics and that exacerbate the progression of DIS-EASE.

The Psychological Mechanism of Stress

In Dr. Claudia Pacheco's writings, lectures, classes, and broadcasts, she routinely points to two basic pathological reactions that human beings "exhibit toward consciousness: fear or anger... which when prolonged eventually give rise to neurosis, psychosis, or organic disease through the stress that is generated by constant tension." She deals with this extensively in her book, *Healing Through Consciousness*.

It is not the "stressor" itself that produces stress-related afflictions. In fact, in certain immediate contacts with a stressor, like when physically threatened, a "fight or flight" reaction may be appropriate. However, prolonged stressful reactions weaken the immune system and lead to all kinds of body/mind afflictions. Dr. Pacheco teaches that these reactions are attitudes that an individual may, or may not, adopt toward consciousness, which you can learn to recognize and deal with, in self and others:

1. In the face of an error or a feeling of envy, predominantly depressive individuals react with fear and attempt to escape in widely diverse ways, ... usually passive, inactive.

2. The paranoid type of individuals are those who, when faced with the consciousness of a frustration or a feeling of envy, react with anger by attacking, hating, or fighting.

A third group includes those who mix the two types of reaction: attack and escape.

It is well known among endocrinologists that anger releases norepinephrine (noradrenalin) and adrenalin into the blood stream, while fear triggers the secretion of acetylcholine and adrenalin. However, "It is not our hormones that cause us to feel anger or fear, but rather the emotions of anger and fear that elicit reactions in certain regions of the brain, commanding the secretion of specific hormones. It is the same with love: when we accept our true feeling, which is affection, our whole body functions in harmony."[40]

Dr. Pacheco speaks of another attitude that triggers the release of hormones; it is that of fantasizing, which can overstimulate the hormonal system, whether the fantasies are sexual or not. "Because of his inverted attitude, the human being sees truth as something aggressive and destructive to himself; and because he wishes to preserve the fantasy of his own perfection, he reacts against any spark of consciousness that contradicts this fantasy.[41]

We have only to look honestly at our own lives to determine whether we are living too much in fantasy or escaping from an accurate perception of ourselves. To what extent are we accustomed to escape by over-indulging ourselves in an array of distractions, including reading, travel, addiction, overeating, chasing sex, money, and social status, etc.? These are signs of prolonged inconscientized reactions to stressors.

In this context, conscientization is a key to self-introspection and a prime factor in a Soul-Over-Mind orientation to the prevention, treatment, and healing of DIS-EASE. It is helpful, not hurtful, when you are being truthful, not suppressive, about your thoughts, words, and deeds. As such, *A.T.* is a testimony to the power of the age-old axioms, "To thine own self be true" and "Know the truth and the truth shall set you free." In this context, being truthful or honest enhances one's ability to know the absolute truth.

Another consciousness-related reason as to why Analytical Trilogy may work so well is how it unearths underlying patterns of actions, emotions, and behavior in a way that relates directly to the science of cosmology from a Soul-Over-Mind perspective. Cosmology views the human being as a spirit, incarnating (and experiencing DIS-EASE) and then ascending the planes of existence (healing), through an array of bodies that are related to these planes, in a process of creation from no-thing to manifestation and then a journey back to the source. You will find that the DIS-EASE conditions you "create" and then heal mirror this process.

CHAPTER 4

DIS-EASE, Cosmology, the Process of Creation, and the Science of the Soul

Explains the metaphysical process of creation from idea to material manifestation, how the evolution of DIS-EASE conditions in one's life mirrors this process, and a scientific means by which to have first-hand "religious" or spiritual experience as a means of healing.

Cosmology, in part, explains the metaphysical process whereby the human being, as a spirit, incarnates or is born into this world and whose spirit eventually ascends back to the source. In this process, humans experience various planes of existence and an array of bodies correspond to these planes. **The onset of DIS-EASE mirrors this progression of creation, from idea to material manifestation; however, a Soul-Over-Mind, healing-through-consciousness orientation can reverse this process**, leading to remediation, problem resolution, progress on the road to spiritual ascension, or reduced suffering. The kind of "scientist" who is concerned with this journey, from a scientific point of view, is the mystic. Before getting into the specifics of cosmology, it furthers to examine its relationship to mysticism and religion.

Mysticism and Organized Religion

The mystic is a human being whose role is to guide and assist those souls who yearn for a personal, more conscious, scientific relationship and union with their Creator, while experiencing peace and ending suffering on earth.

The mystic's purpose is not to form a new religion, reform society, or focus on material prosperity, although the latter can be a byproduct in the lives of those in tune with the mystical path. And although there have been mystics evolving out of the traditions of Christianity, Judaism, Islam, Buddhism, Hinduism, Protestantism, Catholicism, etc., MYSTICISM ITSELF IS NOT A RELIGION (**No doubt there have also been unrecognized mystics growing out of the indigenous cultures and traditional religions of the developing countries of the world, unknown to those focused on the major well-known conventional religions.)

It is beyond the scope of this book to detail a comparative analysis of religious and spiritual teachings and paths. Suffice it to say that the mystics are those who, in this world and throughout history, have dedicated their lives to first-hand experience of the Beyond, and who have shared their experiences via various scriptures, writings, and the oral tradition. Such enlightened ones are also called saints, sages, and saviors, often in whose names thousands of denominations have sprung up like mushrooms.

Myths About the "East"

Mysticism is most commonly known as having evolved out of the so-called "Eastern" religions, such as Hinduism, Buddhism, Jainism, Sikhism, Taoism, Shinto, Confucianism, and East Asian Buddhism. However, this feeds a common misconception about the "East." First, let's get straight what the "East" really is. If you travel WEST from New York City towards California, eventually you will wind up in Asia or what people commonly call the "East." The East is not a fixed geographic location. Mundanely it is the direction in which the earth rotates, such that the sun rises in the east.

From a mystical point of view, the East is what Jesus called the "Single Eye," which mystics have called the "Third Eye," the "door" to your world inside, or as religions teach, "the Kingdom of Heaven" within; it is where the "sun" of enlightenment rises inside on your conscious spiritual journey to the home of your soul.

As Jesus said, "The light of the body is the eye: if therefore thine eye be single, thy whole body shall be full of light" (Matthew 6:22-23 KJV).

The ordinary citizen does not have to practice any conventional religion in order to accept that within them there is a faculty that is a key to wisdom, intuition, and higher consciousness. To truly understand mysticism, one doesn't have to adopt a conventional religion or change one's existing faith or notion of spirituality. In fact, you profit by going deeper into the universal roots of your beliefs or faith.

The Real "Religion" and House of Worship

A cursory look at the word "religion" itself takes it beyond the dogma of organized religion, although you can find its deeper meaning in various scriptures. The word "religion" comes from the Latin root, "re-ligare;" for example, re- (again, back) + ligare or "to connect," to bind back again one's spirit essence to that which created and sustains it. It is turning one's attention inward in order to "worship in spirit and in truth," to enter the "kingdom of heaven" inside and reconnect in consciousness to the Most High. Thus, the real church, mosque, synagogue, or temple is inside the human body wherein the mystic enjoins the seeker to traverse. This is what mystics teach as a way to deal with the issues of everyday life, while at the same time, seeking to gain knowledge of self and one's purpose for being in this world. And it is a reason they place so much emphasis on the practice of meditation.

To repeat: the mystic is concerned with those souls who yearn for a personal relationship with the divine so that they can find peace and harmony inside of themselves.[42] From a scientific point of view, they urge seekers to perform their own experiments in order to realize the truth and apply it to their everyday lives and well-being, and to their efforts to grow spiritually. In this respect, the Science of the Soul goes beyond some of the dogmas and doctrines promulgated by many theologians whose main focus is "Theo" — "logy," the study of God, versus first-hand experience of the divinity, which requires a practice that penetrates to the universal principles underlying one's spiritual or faith tradition and practice.

<u>The Science of the Soul and the Universality of All Religions</u>

In order to better understand the genesis and remediation of DIS-EASE as it relates to Soul-Over-Mind or spirituality, it helps to examine an approach to spirituality that acknowledges the underlying unity of the various religious and spiritual orientations extant or existent. According to Sant Kirpal Singh, a mystic and scholar whose interfaith consciousness was internationally recognized at the *1974 World Conference on Unity of Man*,[43] which featured hundreds of religious, political, and social leaders and delegates, from India and about 30 countries from around the world:

> "Spirituality ... is the science of the soul." It "describes the spiritual journey with its wealth of spiritual planes and sub-planes, the spiritual powers, and possibilities, and their intrinsic worth. Spirituality discloses what the holy Word is and how to commune with It, tells us that the ultimate goal is Self-realization and God-realization, or the union of the soul with the Over-soul, and teaches how it can be achieved.[44]

The Science of the Soul and first-hand experience of the divinity go beyond theology to "apotheosis," which is a way of BEING more Godlike. This idea did not originate in the Western world. "The Ancient Egyptians ... regarded the human body as a prison house of the soul, which could be liberated from its bodily impediments through the disciplines of the Arts and the Sciences, and advanced from the level of a mortal to that of a God."[45]

This is actually consistent with Christian scriptures which teach that the soul essence of the human being is "made in the image of God." As Jesus said, "...is it not written in your law, I said, Ye are gods?" (John 10:34 KJV). Obviously, this does not mean that this person or ego of ours is or should claim to be God, but that the human being should strive to manifest the goodness, truth, and beauty of the Creator, being true to its essential qualities as inherent in the soul or spirit.

Unfortunately, however, human beings often suffer a Mind-

Over-Soul "Theomania," which is a way of their ego envying God or seeing their person as being Godlike; this is a way of perverting our "free" will, which is really only free to do good, in concert with the goodness, truth, and beauty of the Creator. Yes, it is true that we can be creative in the sense of thinking of something, especially material things, and attracting it into our lives. But can we, in identifying with and manifesting through the ego/mind and senses of perception, actually create a blade of grass or a grain of sand, much less the life force of a human soul?

A common theme running through most spiritual teachings is that the main cause of humanity's problems is this undue attachment to the material side of life and a profound lack of knowledge of SELF whose essence is divine. On the walls of the great pyramids of Kemet (Egypt), the ancients enjoin, "man know thyself," teaching that the human being is not, in essence, the "suits of clothing" that we wear in the form of our array of "bodies" and earthly material adornments.

As "individuals," part of us is 'indivisible," the immortal spiritual essence, and part of us is "dual," the mortal material body/mind worn by our essence. In other words, at the root of the DIS-EASEs of humankind is a disconnection with the life-giving part of our being. **However, the Science of the Soul teaches that when we are able to raise our awareness beyond body/mind consciousness, we can avail ourselves of what they call "divine revelations," which serve as nourishment for the soul and a source of healing.** There is a way to achieve this, which is the essence of Soul-Over-Mind, and which shall be further elucidated later in the book.

Healing and Divine Revelations

"...the 'food' which the inner revelations convey is described as conscious and as the nourishment for the soul..."[46] Those revelations convey divine wisdom to the soul and enlighten it. Such a soul receives direct guidance from God, which gradually replaces the limited decisions on the level of the human mind, a perfect example of Soul-Over-Mind.

43

"The divine revelation of light and sound brings forth, in an instant, new divine manifestations for our devotion. The divine manifestations, the conqueror of evils, guide us into the divine gate inside, there providing the conscious, eternal food for the soul."[47]

Sages teaching and practicing the Science of the Soul call these divine revelations, "Naam," which roughly equates to what various religions call the Holy Spirit or the manifestation of a Higher Power or "Intelligence," the ultimate source of healing. These divine revelations reveal themselves to humans in the form of inner light, sound, and *soma* (bliss).

As the creative Power-of-God, "The inner sound has also been developed as a spiritual path or reference point in almost all the religions, traditions, and philosophies worldwide. It has been said that it goes by the following names in these various scriptures and philosophical works:[48]

- AUM, Naad, Akash Bani and Sruti in the Vedas
- Nada and Udgit in the Upanishads
- Akshar in the Bhagavad Gita
- The music of the spheres taught by Pythagoras
- Sraosha by Zoroaster
- Kalma and Kalam-i-Qadim in the Qur'an
- Word and Water of Life in the Bible
- The Divine Wine and HU by the Sufis
- Hari Ras and Amrit by Saints and Mystics
- Naam, Akhand Kirtan and Sacha Shabd in the Guru Granth Sahib
- Logos in Greek and Hebrew metaphysics
- Kneph, in the Medu Neter (Kemetic or Egyptian Language)

Being an emanation from the Supreme Being, Naam reveals the divine will to human beings, and as food is nourishment for the body, revelations of Naam serve as nourishment for the soul. It is also said to be a source of healing on all levels, doing so by:

44

- Washing the soul of conditioning and impressions that impede one's spiritual growth, and that are taken in through the eyes, the ears, the senses, the mind, and emotions,

- Providing ongoing wisdom, inspiration, guidance, and control that enables humans to better manifest the divine virtues preached by all spiritual paths and religions,

- Serving as a medicament that reduces stress and precipitates psychical and physical healing, and

- Cultivating inner peace and reducing suffering, so that humanity is better able to handle the ups and downs of living in his journey to higher achievement, fulfillment, and realization.

The way to gain access to these divine revelations in order to avail us of their healing power will be covered later in the book. Understanding and practicing the science of feeding on divine revelations to nourish the soul, the life-giving part of our being, is a key to transcending from a Mind-Over-Soul orientation to Soul-Over-Mind. As one saint, Sant Kirpal Singh, says:

> **Understanding and practicing the science of feeding on divine revelations to nourish the soul, the life-giving part of our being, is a key to transcending from a Mind-Over-Soul orientation to Soul-Over-Mind.**

"A healthy mind in a healthy body" is a well-known aphorism, and both derive their health and vigor from the soul; and if the soul is not provided with an adequate supply of nourishing and appropriate food-stuff the whole system, physical and mental, will be paralyzed. Soul is a Conscious entity and must, therefore, feed freely on Love, Life, and Light, the three essentials of Greater Consciousness. (i) Naam, or Word, is the panacea for all ills … bodily ailments like disease, sickness, old age, etc.; … or ills coming on of themselves, like accidents, storms, and earthquakes, etc. … or mental ills, like desires and fascinations of the world, anger, greed and attachments, etc. Naam is the sovereign remedy for all ills."[49]

While it is taught that the ultimate access to divine revelations comes in higher forms of spiritual practice, guided by enlightened ones who have "graduated" or completed the path to this "celestial music," it is possible for the average human being to get a "taste of this honey," so to speak. In fact, saints teach that the melodious sounds in higher states of meditation are the source of the development of the musical instruments we play and the sounds they make, which are accessible to us. Meaning, we are all endowed with a life-force, spiritual essence, and consciousness, which is our connection to the divine and its healing. Once, a seeker asked a saint why we need to cultivate the spiritual path, since admittedly, according to spiritual teachings, both God and Soul are already inside of each and every human being. The saint said, "That's true," but the problem is, they haven't met one another."

The Chains of "Evil"
When a human being does not realize who he/she is, in essence, an immortal divine spirit, not the mortal material bodies, one is susceptible to be ruled and manipulated by the ego/mind and material desires, thus precipitating DIS-EASE in one form or another. **For the saint or sage, anything that veers you away or limits you from striving toward union with the divine is "evil,"** because according to them, the ultimate purpose of life is to realize your divinity. However, the evil forces don't want to lose control of one soul, even if it means entrapping the soul in the gold chains of fame and fortune, or the iron chains of obscurity,

discredit, and destitution.

On the other hand, the wise person learns how to reverse course and tread the Soul-Over-Mind path towards the healing and resolution of DIS-EASE. To do so, it pays to have a more detailed understanding of the cosmological progression of creation, from idea to material manifestation. One spiritual system which provides a very detailed map of this path from the unmanifest to the manifest and the return to the unmanifest is the Kabbalah "Tree of Life."

Kabbalah, The Tree of Life and the Process of Creation

The Jewish Kabbalah is a mystical teaching of how the universe was created and the relationship between the infinite, eternal dimension of being and the finite dimension of the Creation. In line with our thesis that the DIS-EASE is the cure, **"The Kabbalah emphasizes that obstacles and challenges are guideposts to our true purpose in the world.** They are stepping-stones to genuine transformation for each of us as individuals, and through us, for humanity as a whole."[50]

One particular feature of the Kabballah is what is called the "Tree of Life," consisting of a schematic series of ten progressive spheres or "sephiroth," which correspond to, 1) the unmanifested spiritual realms giving rise to the planes of existence and the "bodies" of human beings, from the mental/causal to the physical, and 2) the process of creation from "no-thing" to physical manifestation.

Consistent with the cosmology of the Tree of Life, in the process of human beings creatively manifesting results in their lives by positive thinking and the law of attraction, physical manifestation takes place in a certain sequence of Creation. Ideas at the root of physical conditions are like software on thumb drives in a computer. They can be useful and nourishing or infected with viruses. Fortunately, we can remove the infected programming of debilitating ideas, thoughts, and emotions at the root of the ills we suffer. And we can reach into an infinite source of inspiration inside in order to cultivate more self-actualizing ideas, thoughts, emotions, and lifestyle inputs.

As it regards creation, let us, for example, take the simple case of the inspired "creation" of a chair in antiquity, spurred by a person who was tired of standing but wanted an alternative to the available, uncomfortable seats:

PLANES/BODIES	CREATIVE PROCESS
1. SPIRITUAL PLANES/ SOUL, Infinite, Divine Source of Creation,	SOURCE OF INTUITION **Inspiration,**
2. CAUSAL PLANE/BODY	IDEA **of Sitting**
3. MENTAL PLANE/BODY	CONCEPT **of a Rocking Chair**
4. ASTRAL PLANE/BODY	VISION (blueprint, charged with emotion) **Of a Rocking Chair**
5. PHYSICAL PLANE/BODY	PHYSICAL MANIFESTATION **Production of The Rocking Chair**

Inconscientized "Creation"

DIS-EASE, too, mirrors this process of creation. As the ancients teach, "As above, so below… the human being is the microcosm of the macrocosm." Humans are too often unaware of how they are unwittingly "creating" by identifying with seed ideas planted within them that may out-picture in his physical world. From a Soul-Over-Mind, DIS-EASE-is-the-Cure perspective, physical symptoms or conditions, if *conscientized* rather than suppressed, denied, distorted, or overlooked, are designed to make us conscious of the underlying emotional, mental, and idea patterns at the root of the conditions. Often it takes the attendant pain or discomfort to make us pay attention.

As such, physical symptoms or conditions are only the tip of the iceberg. They are manifestations arising from a chain of causation, from idea to form. Merely suppressing or eliminating physical symptoms is akin to mowing grass. The grass keeps growing back unless you starve it at its roots. To "cure" or remedy physical conditions you must conscientize, which is a way of disengaging the life-giving energy from the underlying body/mind patterns which embody the DIS-EASE; you must deprive DIS-EASE conditions of:

> **Humans are too often unaware of how they are unwittingly "creating" by identifying with seed ideas planted within them that may out-picture in his physical world.**

1. " E A R T H " / PHYSICAL—the "soil" housing physical symptoms and habits

2. "WATER"/ASTRAL—the emotions and inner images that feed the conditions

3. "AIR"/MENTAL—the thoughts that affirm the conditions

4. "FIRE"/CAUSAL—the ideas at the root of physical conditions that ignite the process

These DIS-EASE-producing ideas that nest within us can be seeded willfully or unintentionally by negative or demonic spirits. The very process of conscientizing rather than suppressing or denying the symptoms, on the physical, emotional, mental, and idea level of our being, is curative and frees the life-giving spiritual energy to be redirected to wisdom, healing, and problem solving, by opening us up to divine inspiration.

NOTE: To conscientize is to neither suppress nor indulge. It is to pay bare attention to, similar to when you take a brief glance at the time on your watch. Or what Buddhists do in a technique of concentration called "Satipaṭṭhāna," wherein you, the "know-er," merely glance at, not indulge, your drifting thoughts, which are the "known." This Buddhist practice of mindfulness aims to lead to detachment and liberation. It is related to the Analytical Trilogy processes of Interiorization and Conscientization and ul-timately leads to the spiritual practice of meditation. More spe-cific details about how this works and what you can do about it is covered later in the book.

All of the aforementioned chapters lead us directly to an ex-amination of a modality called "Soul Therapy." It is a way to ig-nite the healing of DIS-EASE by engaging the client in a process of conscientizing the underlying body/mind patterns at the root of DIS-EASE symptoms, based on the "disease-is-the-cure" model of holistic health, the law of attraction, the Science of Analytical Trilogy, and the cosmology of the Science of the Soul. As such, it is a Soul-Over-Mind modality that guides the client in retracing and reversing DIS-EASE, by tracing the path of suppression until its roots are discovered and released.

CHAPTER 5

DIS-EASE, SOUL-OVER-MIND,
and Soul Therapy

*Explains the process of guiding clients in going inside and get-
ting in touch with underlying habits/behaviors, and mental, emotional patterns at the root of the DIS-EASE issues and problems
they experience—all in relation to the consciousness and lessons
that the conditions have been designed to teach them. It includes
the concrete benefits of Soul Therapy as a complementary healing modality featuring the elevation of Soul-Over-Mind.*

Soul Therapy is really psycho-spiritual coaching and consulting. That is, its job is to promote healing and remediation by, 1)
guiding the client in opening up and conscientizing the truth of
what is going on inside of them in relation to the presenting issues, but also 2) educating them about the process, in order to
speed up remediation and self-mastery. **Ideally, like in any effective intervention, clients who most profit from Soul Therapy are those who are committed to being truthful and honest
in engaging in a dialectic with the therapist.** Ultimately, it is
knowing the truth that "sets them free."

The Soul Therapy Process

Generally, in-person sessions are more intense or effective,
although sessions for individuals can be held over the telephone
or on digital media. Simulating Sigmund Freud's technique of
the client lying down on a couch, although not mandatory, is ef-

fective where possible, in relaxing the client and helping them to interiorize. Where media is used, the client is advised to sequester themselves in a private room, undisturbed, with no media save the phone or platform used to converse with the therapist. Preferably, they should be lying down or sitting comfortably with hands free, using a headset, if possible. The session always begins with the therapist taking the case, i.e., the client brings up anything that concerns them. Invariably, it will be a symptom or condition of body, mind, or persistent circumstances that are chronic, recurring, and attendant with some degree of upset.

- **The therapist patiently allows the client to spontaneously vent details of the conditions, symptoms, issues, or problems of their concern**—interjecting only for questions of clarification. Then the therapist begins to elicit how the client perceives the symptoms, i.e., their habitual reactions, emotions, thoughts, and ideas related to or about the conditions.

- **The therapist will point out when the client is making faulty associations (inversions),** or when the client tells you what they think when asked what they feel. The therapist also uses spontaneous associating to help clients see the relationship between the conditions they face and the thoughts and ideas (especially errors) that they have been suppressing, denying, distorting, or the details of which they have been overlooking.

- **The therapist may educate the client about the universal principles of cosmology and the process of creation** in relation to the development of the DIS-EASE conditions for which they seek remediation (**being sure to respect the client's beliefs about metaphysical issues.)

- **Once the client begins to realize what is really at the root of the issues they face, the therapist guides them**

in letting go or getting in contact with the higher consciousness (or message) that the conditions are designed to bring to the client. Whereas the session begins by moving up the "planes" and "bodies" of the organism, from the physical to the spiritual dimension of the issues, it ends with moving down from the higher consciousness to healing ideas, thoughts, feelings, and physical effects.

The therapist will always finish by eliciting from the client what they have taken away or learned from the session in their own words. Following this, the therapist will send the client summary notes of the session, and if they wanted it recorded, to a link for the playback. Sometimes the therapist will suggest homework assignments - i.e. readings, references, etc. to follow-up. After a final session, the therapist reviews the extent to which the expected outcomes have been realized.

To summarize: in the process of Soul Therapy, as clients conscientize the ideas at the root of the DIS-EASE symptoms they suffer, through a continuing dialectic, the client comes to realize the higher consciousness that the DIS-EASE is bringing to them. This leads to more enlightened, spontaneous idea associations or intuitions, thoughts, emotions, and often physical gestures, that cap off the Soul Therapy session.

NOTE: The physical gestures act as an "anchor," in the language of NLP,[51] (Neuro-linguistic programming). It embodies the

> **To summarize: in the process of Soul Therapy, as clients conscientize the ideas at the root of the DIS-EASE symptoms they suffer, through a continuing dialectic, the client comes to realize the higher consciousness that the DIS-EASE is bringing to them.**

consciousness realized in the session and can be used to replicate that awareness, all of which is a trigger for healing. **In other words, every time the DIS-EASE issues come up in the life of the client, they can use the anchor as "MEDICINE," to put them in touch with the consciousness that the DIS-EASE symptoms are designed to bring to them. Thus, the DIS-EASE BECOMES THE CURE, OR "MEDICINE, if the truth about it is conscientized and faced, instead of suppressed, denied, censored, distorted or withheld.**

ASCENSION: Description of a Typical Soul Therapy Session for an Individual

This process of reversing DIS-EASE conditions is like peeling off the layers of an onion. It may take several sessions and collaborative interventions. Following is a simplified example of a typical Soul Therapy session which can be conducted for an individual. Below is an outline of an actual case in which the client shared their account of the DIS-EASE symptoms and the therapist elicited their perceptions about it, in order to ascend from consciousness of the depths of the DIS-EASE to consciousness of the heights of remediation.

ASCENSION PROCESS
Starting from "the hand you are dealt" or the Presenting Problem or issues
The client is stuck at 35 pounds overweight.
Client describes in detail the related DIS-EASE symptoms, conditions, conditioning, and shaping factors. One by one, the therapist then elicits the client's reactions, feelings, and thoughts about the presenting problem, including spontaneous free association to get at the idea at the root of the DIS-EASE.

	BODIES	UNDERLYING PATTERNS
		(Inner perceptions that are suppressed, denied, distorted, or overlooked, to one degree or another)
4.	PHYSICAL	HABITS AND REACTIONS **Stuck, unfocused, over-intellectualizing**
3.	EMOTIONAL	FEELINGS **Frustrated**
2.	MENTAL	THOUGHT ASSOCIATIONS, CONCEPTS **Lacking in discipline**
1.	CAUSAL	IDEA, PRINCIPLE **Being an unpleasant, tiresome, disgusting burden**

0.	SPIRITUAL	HIGHER CON-SCIOUSNESS GLEANED
		The need for 360 degrees of consciousness, awakening to all in the universe, to be in sync with it, so that it can help and empower you, and give you the energy and the heart to be who you really are.
		(NOTE: the client spontaneously raised hands to heart and felt an uplifting energy in the chest area; this was to serve as an anchor (NLP) to reproduce that consciousness whenever the symptom of being stuck at overweight comes up)

In the example above, the client has been unwittingly identifying with (but not acknowledging):

- a poor self-image (as if the mortal self or person is the true SELF), Leading to…

- Suppression of thoughts of being undisciplined (which he could easily recognize in others) and feelings of being frustrated.

- Upon reflection, the client may have believed that it's simply being overweight that has caused him to feel stuck, frustrated, and lacking in discipline. However, experience teaches us that being overweight is a symptom, and what has really given rise to being stuck, frustrated, and associated with lacking in discipline, is his unconsciously identifying with the idea in himself of being unpleasant, tiresome, disgusting and a burden, as if that is his true identity, an idea operating, but of which he has suppressed the consciousness.

The Role of Projection

The question is, where did this idea arise from? Often the client will believe it has been caused by his parents and upbringing or the behaviors of others in his life. However, **the soul therapist reveals that however true might be the client's assessment of his parent's behavior (or the conditions and behaviors of others that the client focuses on in session), the question is, why did he attract them?** The truth is that he may have attracted those parents and their behavior to expose conditioning that may be related to his genetics and conditioning at birth (which the saints relate to karma); or it may further be a result of clients' ongoing thoughts, words, and deeds exercised via their free will.

For the therapist, the client's reaction to or blaming of others, even if what one sees in others is true, can reveal a lot about the client. When clients perpetually attract certain conditions or obsess with and seem disproportionately upset by the behavior of others, it is often a sign that they are projecting truths within themselves that they may be suppressing and denying. In her landmark book, *You can Heal Your Life*, author Louise L. Hay speaks on this:

> "If you find yourself saying, "Everyone always does such and such to me, criticizes me, is never there for me, uses me like a doormat, abuses me," then this is YOUR PATTERN. There is some thought in you that attracts people who exhibit this behavior. When you no longer think that way, they will go elsewhere and do that to somebody else. You will no longer attract them"[52]

From a Soul Therapy point of view, the thought could be part of a mindset that you actually came into this world with. And when you conscientize that thinking and let it go, the people who exhibit that behavior will go away or you will be able to deal with them with less suffering or co-dependence.

It is not always the case that the ideas at the root of a client's DIS-EASE conditions are "negative." Sometimes the person is suppressing and denying ideas that reflect the positive aspect of their being, something the ego habitually may do because of its envy of the Creator or its qualities. **In any case, when the client conscientizes the truth of the ideas at the root of his/her DIS-EASE symptoms, they normally open up to some higher wisdom or consciousness, and ideas, thoughts, emotions, and physical release associated with that consciousness.**

As souls we attract the people, environments, and experiences designed to bring consciousness to us and to develop us spiritually. Thus, the problems and obstacles, the DIS-EASE, is the cure. The solution is to conscientize, to stop denying, suppressing, distorting, or overlooking the truth and awareness of what has been going on inside and outside of us. What does this accomplish? To understand it conceptually, it helps to have a grasp of its relationship to cosmology and the cosmological structure of the human being.

The Cosmology of "Being" According to Soul Therapy and the Science of the Soul

As stated earlier, Soul Therapy acknowledges the existence of a Supreme Creator or Higher Intelligence, the qualities of which are Omnipotence: all-powerful, Omnipresence: everywhere, and Omniscience: all-knowing.

GOD, CREATOR SUPREME BEING HIGHER INTELLIGENCE	
Positive Pole Holy Spirit Saints	Negative Pole Universal Mind Satan
HUMAN BEINGS	
Spirit, Soul	Ego
Consciousness	Mind

PHYSICAL BODY

- In manifesting the Creation, the Supreme Being has brought forth what is called the **Holy Spirit**, which has the same essence as the Creator. Many faith traditions recognize that highly evolved and enlightened human beings have and can manifest the **"positive pole"** of the Creation, the embodiment of the Holy Spirit or the "Word made flesh" that dwells among men. This same consciousness is latent but not yet realized in the ordinary human being.

- Also Created is a *Universal Mind* that rules over the mortal realms including the causal, mental, astral, and physical planes, under the management of what various religious and spiritual traditions see as a Principality called "the Devil," or "Lucifer," the "negative" pole of Creation. This entity doesn't want to lose control over one soul, nor does it want the soul to recognize who they really are and where their true home is, from where they originated. It operates according to the unyielding laws of cause and effect, sowing and reaping. In this context, **"evil" is anything, whether it be good deeds or bad deeds, that turns the soul away from its inevitable reconnection to its Creator.** So, one can be charitable, rich and famous, or criminal, poor and infamous and be subject to evil.

- **The Holy Spirit operates in the higher immortal spiritual planes, as well as throughout creation** in the causal, mental, astral, and physical planes. One metaphor shared by saints is that God, the "Ocean" sends the Holy Spirit "River" to carry the Spirit/soul "Drop" back to the Ocean.

- **The soul or spirit within the human being,** as various scriptures attest to, is "made in the image of God." That is, its essence is immortal. It never dies and it operates via consciousness.

- **Within the human being there is also an ego operating through the mind and the senses of perception.** However, the ego/mind, the senses, and the physical body are subject to dissolution or mortality.

- **The problem is that the ego acts as if it is a God because it can "create" in the sense of the law of attraction.** That is, human beings, through their ego/mind, can think of something and attract it into their lives. However, unlike the Supreme Being, the ego/mind can manipulate, but cannot create, a grain of sand or a blade of grass, nor life itself. Thus, the ego becomes envious (Theomanic) because its "creations" pale in the face of the magnificence of the Creator of all. As pointed out in the section on Analytical Trilogy, this is a tremendous burden to bear, the ego trying to live up to being a creator without realizing the source of the creation. Therein lies the reason, as pointed out in Analytical Trilogy, for the chain of envy, inversion, and inconscientization leading to stress, neurosis, psychosis, or DIS-EASE.

When clients acknowledge the truth of this, it makes it easier for them to forgive others, recognizing that one has within them the power to have created and to create their own destiny, and they need not wait to be liberated by others.

Truthfulness is the Currency of Soul Therapy

The first, and perhaps most important, thing to understand is that in any therapeutic modality, whether it be in the field of psychology, general counseling, organizational development, physical healing modalities, problems of all kinds, and in all sectors of society, truthfulness is the most important medium of exchange. Why? Because **cosmologically, truth is synonymous with consciousness, love, spirit and the Creator, all of which are eternal.** From a therapeutic point of view, however, it is most important to conscientize and be truthful about oneself; spouting "truth" to others can be harmful if not guided by divine insight.

In Soul Therapy, it's a simple formula:

- There is a Supreme Being or reality that has created the human being and the entire creation,

- The divine spirit within the human being is the life force and source healing within it, and

- Consciousness is the faculty that the spirit manifests in order to engage the world.

Therefore, when human beings inconscientize, suppress or deny consciousness, they are cutting off their connection to their spiritual essence, and therefore, cutting off their connection to the divine. Ultimately, this is the source of all DIS-EASE, whereas

> **Therefore, when human beings inconscientize, suppress or deny consciousness, they are cutting off their connection to their spiritual essence, and therefore, cutting off their connection to the divine. Ultimately, this is the source of all DIS-EASE, whereas conscientizing is the source of all healing.**

conscientizing is the source of all healing.

There are those who would argue that one person's truth is different from another's. Admittedly, absolute truth is often subject to argument. However, acknowledging the truth of proven or self-evident facts contributes to healing and development. For the therapist, what is most important about "truth" is BEING TRUTHFUL, that is, being honest about how you act or react, what you feel, or what you think. This surely gets you closer to absolute truth, because you are engaging consciousness.

Of course, from a cosmological perspective, we have the choice to serve truth, consciousness, and the divine or the negative forces. The purpose of the Soul Therapy approach to analysis is to buttress or reinforce therapy with an understanding and application of the cosmology underlying life and the human being on the planet.

Why Soul Therapy Works

What Soul Therapy does is to promote remediation by exposing the relationship between upsetting conditions and the truth of what we are identifying with inside but unwittingly suppressing, denying, distorting, or overlooking. As one ancient aphorism says, which was pointed out earlier, "Know the truth and the truth shall set you free." In other words, truth and consciousness heals. And that is the main currency of Soul Therapy.

Suppressing truth or consciousness is tantamount to

struggling against reality, against our own being, our real self, and our Creator, which we see as the underlying cause of DIS-EASE. Conversely, being conscious or truthful is embracing and reconnecting to our divinity, opening us up to a taste of inner divine revelations, which, at the highest level, do the following:

- Promote enlightenment by dissolving the impurities and conditioning that mask the light of the soul and impede spiritual development;

- Confer wisdom and intuitive guidance that is not so easily grasped by the mind, the intellect, and ego-based free will;

- Promote the healing of individuals, relationships, organizations, and society; and

- Reduce suffering, thus enabling all to better bear life's inevitable ups and downs.

Specific Soul Therapy Outcomes

During Soul Therapy sessions, the immediate objective is for the client to acknowledge the truth of the ideas, thoughts, emotions, and reactions or habitual behavior and errors that underlie, abet, or may have a causal relationship to the conditions for which the client has sought relief.

Soul Therapy is not a substitute for appropriate conventional medical or other professional consultation. On the contrary, it is complementary to other healing and problem-solving modalities, and is deemed successful if it helps the client to experience one or more of the following outcomes, after a session or series of sessions:

1. LONG-TERM OUTCOMES

   a. **Accelerated healing:** the resolution and/or prevention of prolonged chronic, recurring conditions and problems;

b. **Be better able to find or attract additional professional help best suited to address aspects of their issues:** i.e., more customized, appropriate qualified help for acute and chronic conditions they are experiencing;

c. **More energy to follow remedial regimens:** properly prescribed by competent practitioners or professionals;

d. **More inner peace, less suffering and the will to progress spiritually:** enabling clients to persevere in the process of resolving chronic problems, to the extent they can be remedied, as they go through a necessary healing process.

2. IMMEDIATE OUTCOMES: (during the session)

a. **Physical:** a lighter feeling, as if a burden has been lifted, (often including a measure of immediate relief of presenting physical issues);

b. **Emotional:** calming down, like a balloon releasing air;

c. **Mental:** Clarity and sharpened awareness of inverted or upside-down thinking related to the conditions about which they seek relief;

d. **Causal:** Gaining new intuitive insights and epiphanies, (sometimes an "a-ha" moment); and

e. **Spiritual:** Experiencing a "taste of honey," i.e., inner peace, joy or blissful moments

Soul Therapy as Preparation for Advanced Forms of Higher Healing and Remediation

Soul Therapy, as a form of psycho-spiritual interiorization, or going within through engaging in a dialectical, interactive dialogue, coaching and consulting with clients, is merely preparation for more advanced Self-actualization or Realization. Ultimately, saints advocate that the highest level of healing for a human being is self-mastery, gained by higher forms of spiritual practice, especially meditation, under the guidance of enlightened ones who have already reached or mastered that plateau.

The conscientizing experienced by clients in the process of Soul Therapy (as it is in Analytical Trilogy) is a deepening of the spiritual connection, a pivotal phase at the root of all practical steps toward the prevention, treatment, healing, and remediation, of DIS-EASE. How this paradigm plays out in relationships, organizations, and society is the subject of the next chapter, which concludes with a brief discussion of the application of the Soul Therapy methodology to groups in the organizational context.

CHAPTER 6

DIS-EASE-is-the-Cure in the interpersonal, organizational context

Discusses how the healing of DIS-EASE, in the context of various associations, begins with directly facing and embracing, rather than suppressing, conflict, using the power of mediation and meditation as a spiritually-based approach.

What is true within the individual is no less true within "associations" (relationships, groups or organizations, all of which are organisms or entities in and of themselves.) In them, the pain and upset of conflicts and challenges makes us pay attention to what we may be ignoring or even denying and suppressing. On the other hand, associations as entities can choose to find the time and patience to focus and pay attention without being forced to by conditions. In doing so, such organisms can tap into a tremendous, inexhaustible font of inner resources, valuable assets to utilize in the course of doing business or working out relationships.

"God" or the "Higher Self" in Associations
Associations, like individual human beings, have, and are, more than just their collective human minds or policies, procedures, goals, and objectives. Hereafter, we will refer to this collective as "minds." The essence of an association is that intangible asset within it that uses its "mind" and "body" (human and structural facilities). It is that which is the "knower" (not the known) that sees and hears through the individual and collective

eyes and ears of its populace. A panoramic study of philosophic, religious, and spiritual literature generally finds much agreement that the life-giving principle within all the creation, including associations, is connected to an omnipotent, omniscient, omnipresent reality. Some call it God, Supreme Being, Creator, the All, or a Higher Intelligence.[53]

Whatever this all-expansive reality is, or whatever you choose to call it, there is a spark of this divinity within each and every human being or association as an organism. Some call this spark soul, or spirit, or animus.[54] Whatever you call it, it's generally agreed that it has the same essential qualities of immortality as the "Higher Intelligence." To consciously and willfully access this entity via what we will call the "Higher Self," requires the ability to enter into its domain, first via the "mind," and then beyond the "mind."

The enhanced capacity and will to resolve conflicts, needs, and challenges in route to achieving goals is rooted in our ability to learn how to consciously access the Higher Self and navigate in the realms where it resides, in an effort to connect with a Higher Intelligence of which it is a part, and thereby access all of its inner resources. A cursory look at the challenges, obstacles, problems, and conflicts within associations and entities throughout all sectors of society, underscores the need for a more enlightened approach to preventing, treating, and healing the DIS-EASEs of civilization.

Spirituality—Key to Tapping Inner Planetary Resources

Back in the 1990s, there was a United Nations Non-Government Organization (NGO), A Centre for the World's Religions (ACWR), that conducted meditation instruction and peace forums at the UN in an effort to harness the inner resources of UN delegates, staff, and NGOs, to enhance their work for world peace. ACWR worked under the premise that **we on this planet have more than enough resources to solve the world's problems of war, poverty, and pollution; and the greatest resource we have is within us where peace begins, one person at a time.**

ACWR recognized that, theoretically, religion could be a prime resource for achieving world peace; however, war and conflict is rooted in humanity's inability to see the universal common roots that we share, irrespective of differences in religion, culture, nationality, race, and creed. And the wars and battles inflaming nations and organizations on the planetary body we call earth are macrocosms of the microcosmic conflicts and skirmishes raging within and among people.

From a SOUL-OVER-MIND perspective, it is not necessary for individuals to change their religious or spiritual perspective to employ spirituality and consciousness to resolve DIS-EASE. What helps is to look at the underlying meaning of the word "religion" itself. It comes from the Latin root, "re-ligare", for example, re- (again, back) + ligare or "to connect." Therefore, the essence of religion, as taught in many religions, is to worship in spirit and in truth, to consciously enter the kingdom of heaven inside and reconnect to our Creator or "Higher Intelligence."

In this context, the real church, mosque, synagogue, or temple is more than a building made of bricks and mortar, it is inside the human body, gifted to every human being who make up associations of human beings. However, for associations or organizations to employ universal spirituality to more effectively resolve the 21st century DIS-EASEs that afflict mankind, they must understand and respect the underlying universality of the people working within them.

What Followers of Different Religions Have in Common

What binds together human beings of whatever religious or spiritual perspective is the heartfelt desire to elevate their consciousness, become enlightened, and make contact with the divine essence or life force within them. A cursory look at the labels of the followers of various faiths makes this point:

- MUSLIM: One who is in submission to God.

- BUDDHIST: From "Bodhi," which means awakened and

enlightened—in a state of "Nirvana" or oneness with all, as was the Buddha.

- CHRISTIAN: As from "Christ," the "Messiah" or Messiahs, Aramaic "meshiha," The anointed (of the Lord), or "Khristos," one who answers directly to God.

- TAOIST: As in one who identifies with the "Tao," the "universal life force," or Holy Spirit

- JEWISH: One who praises God, as in Judaism, from Yehudah (i.e. "Judah"), combining "praise" and "God" into one new name.

- HINDU: As "devoted to light as against darkness;" from the word "India" whose Sanskrit name is "Bharat," meaning "Bha" which means light and knowledge. "Rata" means "Devoted," all ultimately meaning, "highly enlightened spiritually."

  NOTE: keep in mind that NONE of the enlightened beings venerated by their followers actually created the religions or thousands of sects established in their names.

The bottom line is that all of us have a life force within us, were created by some force, and have a will and consciousness that differentiates us from lower species. Therefore, whether practicing a particular religion or spiritual path, or choosing to be an agnostic or atheist, it is possible to work together to tap into our inner resources to address the DIS-EASE conditions within self and the associations within which we participate or work.

Associations that are wise will create a safe space that respects and encourages individuals' efforts to: delve more deeply into the universal roots of their own religious, spiritual, or non-religious views of reality; learn how to go within to have one's own direct, firsthand experience of consciousness; and come together with one another in the true spirit of communion to compare notes and discover the universal principles they share, rather than dwell on their differences. But first, associations must directly confront the DIS-EASE or conflicts, obstacles, and challenges faced within, between, and among them.

whether practicing a particular religion or spiritual path, or choosing to be an agnostic or atheist, it is possible to work together to tap into our inner resources to address the DIS-EASE conditions within self and the associations within which we participate or work.

Obstacles to Facing Up to DIS-EASE Conditions in Associations

Resolving conflicts in group or interpersonal settings can be inhibited by legitimate concerns including:

- feelings by individuals that they do not really have much to offer outside of the specifics of their work or relationship role; that their contributions are unappreciated or unwelcome; or that the work or interpersonal environment is not "safe" enough to inspire sharing their feelings and views;

- fears of invasion of privacy;

- concerns about intolerance or harassment because of one's personal lifestyle or spiritual, political, or cultural beliefs and practices;

- apprehension at possible attempts at converting one to other social, cultural beliefs; and,

- fears that one's personal beliefs can be used against them.

This can be especially true in times of economic challenges, and in associations, changes in organizational direction or leadership which may portend significant changes, sometimes arbitrary, in roles. Thus, staff may be faced with the challenge of taking the time to more rigorously clarify and even mediate roles.

At the root of DIS-EASE or conflicts in associations is role ambiguity, which exacerbates struggles between and among individuals to determine who makes the decisions to control and guide the use of shared space and resources.

Mediation of Disputes or roles in organizations is a sort of collective attempt to meditate or concentrate on finding a unifying goal or objective to resolve issues that may have been ignored, suppressed, denied, or even swept under the rug. Often, it is only when fomenting emotions begin to erupt, or DIS-EASE symptoms surface, that the light of awareness (consciousness) is directed to the issues. So, in effect, the DIS-EASE becomes the cure if conscientized rather than suppressed, denied, distorted or overlooked.

Inherent in conflict is energy that can be harnessed and used to heal and solve problems. The DIS-EASE-IS-THE-CURE model discussed earlier applies to associations. In a holistic approach to organizational development, like with an individual, when an entity does not take the time to live more holistically, the organism's inner attempt to eliminate resulting morbific[55] matter is blocked, and disease is both the result and the "cure."[56]

Whether the organism is a human being or an organization, the root energy to heal it from conditions of DIS-EASE is found within it. This energy or life force is always working to evolve and grow the organism and does so with much less discomfort when we identify and cooperate with it.

Interpersonal Associations and Organizations as Organisms

A more in-depth, comprehensive analysis of the organization as a living organism in need of holistic treatment is beyond the scope of this book. However, following is a mindset that associations and organizations can use to further develop in a holistic way, in order to more effectively prevent, treat, and resolve DIS-EASE in their midst:

- There is a collective "life-giving" root healing energy inherent in organizations as is the case with human beings.
- "Holistic" for an organization consists of its non-suppressive, nourishing high ideals and practices, and socially responsible objectives and activities.
- Organizations, like individuals, can choose to adopt non-enervating inputs and processes, both as a matter of routine or to consciously address and treat conflicts or DIS-EASE in its ranks.
- Hering's Law of recurring symptoms regarding homeopathy operates in organizations, too, as mentioned earlier for individuals in the chapter on DIS-EASE-IS-THE-CURE, whereby curative, holistic measures may require associations to work through temporary aggravation of symptoms to move in the direction of curing association ills.
- Through its strategic planning, evaluation, and staff development processes, associations, like individuals, can choose to "conscientize" rather than deny and suppress symptoms of conflict or DIS-EASE.
- Organizations can simulate the principles of SOUL-OVER-MIND through enlightened mediation of conflicts and can encourage or support workers' individual efforts to meditate and incorporate other holistic practices.

Simulating meditation can help organizations to slow down and calm scattered, conflicting systems and interactions in order to access the "soul" of the organization and draw upon or reconnect to its "Higher Intelligence" and mission, to facilitate healing and growth. An examination of a Role Mediation/Clarification model of conflict resolution can aid in developing a

SOUL-OVER-MIND meditation mindset in an organization.

The Cosmogony of Roles in Organizations

There is a direct link between the Role Mediation/Clarification model of organizations and the concept of human beings as entities having a Higher Self which can be realized, and which can unite with a Higher Intelligence.

In human beings, the absolute Higher Intelligence is symbolized by the circle (or *zero*). It represents infinity, eternity, the all, "no-thing," or the full scope of the organization's mission. In the association, as the zero/circle represents the absolute mission or purpose for which the organization incorporates, all that follows must align with that mission.

The point within the circle represents the Higher *Self* of a human being, which is "made in the image" of the Higher Intelligence; the point within the circle of an association represents the prime ideal, *goal,* or aim that drives the entity towards oneness with its mission.

To avoid or resolve conflicts within organizations, the individual roles of workers (their job descriptions) must align with the mission of the organization, as should workers' periodic goals and objectives align with the current goals and objectives of the organization. Conflict results when:

- The mission and goals of organizations are ambiguous or not being followed

- Its action plans and policies, procedures, and behaviors are not in alignment with the mission or goals, or its goals and processes are outdated and not receptive to innovation

- The individual roles and goals of workers and/or departments are ambiguous, not in alignment with the organization's mission/goals or resistant thereto, or

- The mission, goals, and roles of individuals are not in sync with or too far out of alignment with that of the association and mitigate against personal fulfilment

To some extent, normally-occurring conflicts can resolve themselves if the organization has an ongoing holistic approach rooted in a continual process of focusing awareness (Conscientizing) to thereby access the organization's higher Intelligence. Ongoing Role Mediation/Clarification is crucial to this process of awareness. The cosmogony of the circle/zero, in the context of "territorial prerogative"[57] in organizations can help illustrate this principle.

To some extent, normally-occurring conflicts can resolve themselves if the organization has an ongoing holistic approach rooted in a continual process of focusing awareness (Conscientizing) to thereby access the organization's higher Intelligence.

Territorial Prerogative and Conflict in Organizations

Let us look again at the symbol of two circles with a point in each's center, in this case representing workers within an organization (or individuals in a relationship). The circumference symbolizes the boundary of the worker's role (or "territory") within the organization or relationship. The role ideally aligns with organization and corresponding departmental missions, the boundaries of which should be clearly understood and internalized by the worker.

Let us say that that normally the points within the circle represent the workers, calm and centered on the job, with some idea of how to function in their roles or territory. But something comes up causing them to move towards each other's territory. The workers feel threatened or *invaded* and move from their center towards the periphery to meet the challenge.

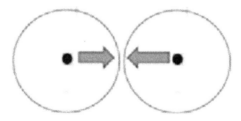

Workers move to meet a threatened invasion of their territory

As both workers move towards the boundaries of their respective circles, let's say the two roles overlap, resulting in a shared space in which it is not clear who controls decisions on how to utilize the resources (time, manpower, material, and finance) in the shared space. *Conflict* is inevitable unless role definition and guidelines are established for how the two roles operate in the shared space.

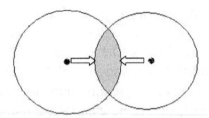

Worker "A"   *Worker "B"*

The more the two engage and negotiate, the less conflict becomes debilitating and the easier it is to resolve conflict and share "space." For example, the more supervisors and managers:

1. Face the DIS-EASE as a curative process rather than suppressing conflict, sweeping it under the rug, or imposing unilateral ego/mind-based directives;

2. "… facilitating what is happening is more potent than pushing for what you wish were happening … Learn to trust what is happening … If there is silence, let it grow; something will emerge. If there is a storm, let it rage; it will resolve into calm." Otherwise, you "might well deprive the group of a very creative struggle."[58]

3. Collaborate with employees to define each role in relation to shared goals, objectives, common or compatible missions, and the process of decision-making;

4. Facilitate, not control the process, and support workers' efforts (like meditation) to operate from their center and/or bring higher wisdom to the periphery in the process of negotiation,

Role Mediation/Clarification should help workers, including management, become conscious of the congruency of organizational and personal mission, goals, and objectives in a way that they can realize the underlying unity to help ease conflict and achieve goals. This process of Role Mediation/Clarification on the organizational level is epitomized by, and can be enhanced by the process of, meditation, a SOUL-OVER-MIND orientation on a personal and group level.

Meditation and Organizational Development

On a personal level, any effort to use meditation to help focus one's role in life in general, or on the job in particular, confronts a shifting, changing mind that seems to have a mind of its own. This is exacerbated by a culture in which a barrage of media and stimuli is specifically designed to capture our attention and divert it outside of ourselves. Music, videos, movies, radio, television, newspapers, magazines, advertisements, food establishments, computers, creature comforts, etc. assault us during every waking hour. So, when do we find the time and energy to sit and meditate?

The process of meditation involves first becoming aware of and slowing down the endless parade of thoughts (often conflicting) barraging the mind. This bombardment of thoughts is called "thought drift." These thoughts and underlying ideas are associated with the conditions and events that we experience in our lives. Hopefully, through the process of meditation, we may be better able to become more aware that:

1. Thoughts are things that have a life of their own;

2. We are not, in essence, our thoughts; rather we are the Higher Self that perceives these thoughts; and

3. The thought patterns occupying our mind space may or may not be serving a higher purpose in our lives.

In advanced stages of meditation one can stop thoughts completely ("lose one's mind") and experience oneself as the Higher Self, devoid of the limitations of body and mind. This is called

Self-Realization. At the highest stages of meditation, the consciousness of Higher Self merges with the Higher Intelligence; the meditator becomes a co-worker with the Higher Intelligence, expressing its essential qualities (while still living in the physical body).[59]

As discussed earlier regarding a DIS-EASE-IS-THE-CURE approach to healing, the association, like the individual, benefits from consciously applying its will to discern what the organism needs and adopts an organizational "diet," lifestyle and culture, or environment, that, to the extent possible, nourishes and supports the organism.

When we fail to properly nourish the organism or tune into its innermost needs, it acts on its own to regain homeostasis. The result is perpetual or chronic conflict, with attendant symptoms of pain and upset that make us pay attention to what we otherwise may have been too deaf, dumb, and blind to perceive.

As is the case with individuals, weaknesses in the formation of the association's "heredity," compounded by toxic environmental factors and a willfully unnatural or enervating work-life culture, overtaxes the organism's ability to eliminate the toxins and harmoniously carry on business. When the organism is overwhelmed and blocked in its efforts to routinely eliminate toxic elements, it leads to an abnormal or heightened effort to detoxify, which the association experiences as conflict or DIS-EASE. Ideally, the most curative intervention is that which assists the organism in this effort to heal itself, as quickly and as efficiently as possible, versus suppression as discussed earlier.

Long-term suppression can evolve a condition from acute to chronic wherein the association may still exist in a relatively pain-free but illusionary state of health. But the organism will be in a much weaker state, operating at less than maximum capacity, its functions and major "organs" weakened, and vulnerable and susceptible to further, more chronic, DIS-EASE. The attendant pain and upset is actually designed to conscientize the association as to what is really going on inside of it, but which it has been to some extent denying and suppressing.

The process of mediation and role clarification described herein can be enriched by the association creating a space in which employees can learn about and practice a universal method of meditation. From a SOUL-OVER-MIND perspective, consciousness or conscientizing is the foundation of meditation, as it is in the modalities of Analytical Trilogy and Soul Therapy described earlier.

Conscientizing and Meditation

Meditation, properly done, is a natural, dynamic form of conscientization that complements the processes of Analytical Trilogy and Soul Therapy, and can eventually, as taught by saints and enlightened sages, serve as a vibrant form of self-analysis. Through it, the individual:

- Becomes conscious of what is actually happening in their sphere of awareness on the mind screen (which one may be suppressing, denying, distorting, or overlooking the truth of); and
- Slows down the mind to the extent of becoming aware of ,and drawn up in consciousness to, the reality beyond the mind, in order to partake of its healing and uplifting properties.

The efficacy of meditation is based on how it relates to the inner functioning of a human being.

The Practical Benefits of Meditation

The ultimate object of meditation is to still the "Indivi-dual's" shifting, changing mortal body/mind—the *dual* part of one's being—in order to access the indivisible, immortal Higher Self. In the process, one may access ideas and thoughts that can help resolve conflicts, meet needs, and enrich goal achievement. In practice, it is more or less common knowledge today, based on anecdotal as well as scientific studies, that meditation has innumerable benefits applicable to the lives of individuals at home, at play, and in the workplace:

- Increased productivity and job satisfaction
- Improved relations at work
- Improved employee health and more positive health habits
- Increased relaxation and decreased stress at work
- Increased stress reduction and relaxation
- Increased memory, comprehension, creativity, perception, and the ability to focus and concentrate
- Increased protection against, or prevention of, cardiovascular disease and other stress-related afflictions, and
- Increased self-actualization, intuition, and peace of mind

These documented benefits of meditation, including stress reduction, healing, and improved concentration, are key factors for success in all material endeavors, let alone pursuit of higher "spiritual" objectives.

In looking at the association as an entity or organism, creating a space in which workers can use down time or staff development time to meditate, can be a productive complement to role clarification and mediation, in order to prevent, treat, and remedy DIS-EASE as it manifests in the association. The appendix outlines a simple technique of meditation and what to expect. Following are some basic principles to help guide the individual and associations in choosing a useful and production method of meditation.

Organizations that encourage or facilitate the practice of meditation will ensure that workers bring more internal renewable resources to bear in fulfilling their missions. In the process, it will help prevent, treat, or remedy, conflicts or DIS-EASE and allow workers to more clearly discern the role of work in the fulfillment of personal goals.

Meditation and Role Mediation/Clarification in organizations both begin with confronting (Conscientizing) conflicting mind-sets and altercations in the workplace. In this context, the conflict or DIS-EASE is the cure—the organism's effort to expose and transcend obstacles that impede its effort to realize individuals' and the association's "Higher Self," ideals, and "Higher Intelligence," or Mission.

We cannot afford to neglect finding the time to facilitate meditation and mediation of role ambiguity in associations. Paying attention to (but not necessarily indulging) inner and outer conflict via meditation and mediation, while constantly returning the focus to one's center or goals, is what slows down or defuses conflicting thoughts and conditions. Meditation and Role Mediation/Clarification enable staff to serve as role models of how to access inner personal and organizational resources to successfully re-educate oneself and others.

Activities at home, in relationships, in organizations, and in society can be enhanced and profitable when all concerned, starting with self, become more self-reliant and resourceful by going within, by mediation and meditation, to resolve conflicts and spur growth.

Meditation and Role Mediation/Clarification can be vital tools in developing a more holistic approach to life and organizational development and are an essential source of "food" that sustains the life of the individual and the association. As such, they are supreme means of cost efficiency in that the *inner* **resources of self and organization are essentially infinite and eminently "renewable," thus ensuring the highest level of goal achievement.**

CHAPTER 7

DIS-EASE and "Foods" That Sustain Life

Explains how to take action and enhance healing through Soul-Over-Mind modalities that capture the essential life energy, through lifestyle, diet, and energy-based modalities.

From a Soul-Over-Mind perspective, truly cultivating wellness requires us to "nourish" every dimension of our being, especially the Spirit. In the face of DIS-EASE, it is imbibing the kinds of "foods" that sustain life and enhance prevention, treatment, accelerated healing, or remediation of DIS-EASE, rather than relying primarily on conventional means of suppressing symptoms. From this point of view, **just as the physical body needs certain kinds of food to thrive, so, too does the spirit and the energetic bodies of humans.** First, let us go into more detail as to what, exactly, the "essential energy" is.

The Essential Energy and Spirit as "Food"

The essential energy is the manifestation of the life force within human beings and the creation. It is the actual source of healing for humankind. Its source is what various religions and teachings have called the "Holy Spirit," which was discussed earlier as "Naam" and various other labels in the different spiritual paths of the world. It is possible via certain forms of meditation to gain direct conscious access to Holy Spirit divine revelations as food or nourishment for the spirit.

What is said to connect the Holy Spirit to the denser bodies of human beings is an "etheric" body within which **there are energy centers in humans that absorb what is called "chi" (qi), or "prana," which is the root "food" for the mortal bodies of human beings**.

The etheric body can be seen by some as the "aura" around the physical body. Moving the body a certain way causes the body to absorb the chi from the air differently and to circulate it differently. Chi is absorbed with every breath you take. The sun is a source of chi also, believe it or not, and a powerful one.[60] (This is why certain exercises and being in tune with nature are so important.)

This chi (or prana) is not just something that feeds the physical body of the human being. It is, in essence, "The infinite, omnipresent manifesting power of this universe [which] evolved everything that we call energy, everything that we call force. It is the Prana that is manifesting as motion; it is the Prana that is manifesting as gravitation, as magnetism. It is the Prana that is manifesting as the actions of the body, as the nerve currents, as the thought force. From thought down to the lowest force, everything is but the manifestation of Prana. The sum total of all forces in the universe, mental or physical, when resolved back to their original state, is called Prana."[61] According to this teaching there is chi or prana in every breath we take, in the ground, in the food, and in the sun, as food that sustains life, if we are able to learn how to imbibe it.

"Foods" That Sustain Life

For an example of a SOUL-OVER-MIND mindset leading to increased relief from chronic DIS-EASE, we can learn from some of what transpired during the 1980s at the height of the AIDS epidemic. A holistic center in Harlem, NY named Daya Associates — Nu Age Center of Harlem, facilitated weekly support groups for people with life-threatening diseases such as cancer, AIDS, multiple sclerosis, etc. Following is what the center discovered about the profile of those who survived and thrived the best:

1. **They consciously deepened their spiritual connection.** Irrespective of their particular religious backgrounds, they sought and practiced ways to tap into the spiritual "food" or life force of their being;

2. **They tended to see the disease, not as a death sentence, but as an opportunity to live life to the fullest.** In this context, they recognized that the disease is actually the cure, in the sense that it is the spirit's attempt to expel toxins and heal the body, and that what is needed is to not just suppress the symptoms, but figure out what the organism is trying to do and work with it.

3. **They incorporated alternative lifestyle and dietary measures as a permanent way of life, and not just a temporary quick fix or silver bullet.** These measures looked at food much more holistically, as "nourishment that sustains life." Thus, they expanded their notion of foods as that which enables the human being to imbibe the actual "essential energy" that heals, prevents illness, and maintains wellness.

Various Sources of the "Essential Energy "as "Food"

This essential energy is basically the life force moving through a human being and the creation. It is made available to humans by direct access via consciousness, and in the form of what is called (chi or prana), the elixir that sustains the heartbeat, breath-

> **This essential energy is basically the life force moving through a human being and the creation. It is made available to humans by direct access via consciousness, and in the form of what is called (chi or prana), the elixir that sustains the heartbeat, breathing, and the organism's ongoing wellness.**

84

ing, and the organism's ongoing wellness. So, what are these foods and how are we to imbibe them?

- **Divine Revelations:** this is nourishment for the soul via direct contact with our source of life or "Holy Spirit." This food is imbibed through:

  o *Silent meditation:* ("Be still and know that I am God."), and **prayer** (gratefulness and glorifying our Creator for the gift of life and mercy):

    "In this dizzying array of medical innovations, meditation requires no medical equipment. Meditation is a medication for the health of the body, mind, and soul. Meditation plays a role in preventive medicine. It has an effect on supplementing medication and speeding recovery. It has a benefit on the emotional and mental state of patients. It has a value when doctors are dealing with patients who are either terminal or who have a life-threatening illness."[62]

  o *Selfless service to humanity:* serving with no thought of personal gain, includes things like tithing:

    The spiritual master Sri Soami Divyanand Ji Maharaj, in His lectures, has said that selfless service is like a "cash transaction;" you get an immediate benefit of progress toward divine revelations and mitigating the karma that impedes progress toward spiritual enlightenment, even if, for one reason or another, the seeker is unable to meditate. In fact, it is more effective in transcending the ego than meditation.

  o *Fellowship:* joining with others in seeking truth.

85

Thus saith the Lord, "For where two or three are gathered together in my name, there am I in the midst of them" (Matthew 18:20 - KJV).

Indian spiritual masters call their fellowship, "Satsang," which literally means "in the company of truth." They teach that the most dynamic such fellowship occurs in the presence of a saint who transmits spiritual energy as one gazes into their eyes. It doesn't matter to them if people blaspheme or slander the circle of Satsang. Masters say that this puts a fence around the gathering into which they only want the presence of sincere seekers after truth.

Much of what constitutes "food that sustains life" is a matter of common sense, which all too often we reject in favor of conventional so-called experts, and which don't require a double-blind study to authenticate. It still makes sense to research the following basic common sense foods to go deeper and/or corroborate and distinguish between conflicting claims as to efficacy. Following are just some tips to help guide your investigation:

- **Sunshine:** being sure to spend some quality time out of doors in the sun and among nature that is nourished by the sun. However, beware of excessive sun worshipping and toxic ingredients in most suntan lotions and sunscreens. Also, look into other sources of vitamin D, not as a substitute but as a supplement. "The Sun can transform your health" and "acts as a magnet in drawing out toxins. When we eat correctly and are detoxified, reasonable exposure to the sun cannot lead to skin cancer."[63]
- **Oxygen** (the elixir of life, it's also the single most important element required in all forms of healing): Spending quality time in the mountains, at the seashore, and in

parks or forests where the greenery gives off life-giving oxygen and imbibing oxygen-rich foods, supplements, and certain deep breathing exercises.

- **Water:** Most of our bodies is made up of water. In fact, dehydration is a major factor in many illnesses. Water is a critical factor in detoxification, lubricating the joints, delivering nutrients to the cells, regulating body temperature, facilitating digestion, etc. It pays to research alternative sources, i.e.., natural live foods containing pure water, and filtered, alkaline, hydrogenated, or ozonated (preferably bottled in glass).
- **Sleep:** Rejuvenating rest, especially after sundown and in a darkened environment. NOTE: "One hour of meditation can give as much relaxation as four hours of sleep. Thus, fifteen minutes of meditation during our work break can give us the rejuvenation of one hour of sleep. Imagine a one-hour nap in the middle of our day. Meditation gives us that rejuvenation."[64]
- **Live**, **Natural Foods** (As much as possible), i.e., foods rich in prana via enzymes, oxygen, and pure water,_
  - *Predominantly or all plant-based, at least 20% live* (uncooked)
  - *Locally grown to the greatest extent possible*
  - *Organic, non-GMO (genetically modified), to the greatest extent possible*
  - *Whole and less processed*
  - *Additive/preservative-free*
  - *Nutritional herbs, homeopathic remedies, and whole food supplements*

NOTE: *Beware of the cosmetics that you put on your body. Many of the additives are toxic and absorbed "eaten" by the body through the skin. Choose cosmetics, including soaps, with natural food ingredients as much as possible.*

- **Periodic Fasting (see the appendix)**: temporarily abstaining from food or from anything in life that you are imbibing that may be causing DIS-EASE symptoms. In doing so, the body begins to heal itself by sending the liberated nerve energy to wherever is in need of healing.

- **Exercise:** Walking, aerobics, swimming, Tai Chi or Qi Gong, Yoga, etc. (all are rich in circulating the prana/chi, sun/fire, oxygen, water, blood, lymph and nerve energy and are a source of massage for the inner organs). These movements stimulate healthy heart functioning and de-toxification. Find one or more that you can commit your-self to.

- **Consciousness-raising and energy-balancing healing modalities:** massage, reflexology, Chinese medicine and acupuncture, Ayurvedics, Reiki, chiropractic medicine, iridology, naturopathy, Analytical Trilogy, Soul Therapy, just to name a few. What many have in common is 1) making psychosomatic correspondences between DIS-EASE symptoms and ways of thinking and emoting, and/ or 2) provide maps of the body and ways to channel heal-ing energy to related organs and structures.

An example is iridology:
  The iris of the eye contains a map of the body such that observing the coloring on different parts of the iris can reveal what is happening in the corresponding parts of the body. There are five main colors in the iris of the eye:

  1. The natural color of the iris
  2. White spots that indicate acute inflammation
  3. Light brown spots that indicate sub-chronic conditions
  4. Dark brown spots that symbolize chronic con-ditions
  5. Black spots that indicate degenerative condi-tions

  As healing progresses, the colors get lighter, as health worsens the spots get darker. It is advisable to complement your conventional laboratory and medical diagnosis with a readout from a competent iridologist, many of whom also are knowledge-able of herbs, supplements, and alternative remedies. **Sometimes, an iridological consultation can reveal latent conditions that have not yet shown up in conventional tests and diagnoses.**

- **Aesthetics:** cultivating higher forms of beauty and balance in the arts, visual, performing, and music, is an important element in the treatment of DIS-EASE. The brilliant Brazilian psychotherapist, Dr. Norberto Keppe, in his lectures and treatment of psycho-socio pathology and psychosomatic medicine, says that aesthetics is the origin of philosophy, all of science, psychology, sociology, and even engineering and physics."

  Not only can true art and aesthetics expose pathology, he says, "The arts make the connection for the human being between the physical, this material world here, and transcendence."

  Keppe considers the genuine artist, who is often attacked by the envious, as being "a superior being; no one throws stones at a dried-up tree, only at that which bears fruit." It's no wonder in authoritarian governments, funding for the arts is the first to go.

"Foods That Sustain Life" in the Institutional Setting

The following elements outline how companies can better facilitate the feeding of "foods that sustain life" to workers. It is drawn from a chapter authored by yours truly, Leonard Burg, in a chapter entitled, "Profit by Consciousness of Spirituality in the Workplace" in the best-selling publication, *The Better Business Book, Volume 2*. The book features 100 authors each sharing their most valuable business lesson.[65]

Within corporate America there is an increasing awareness of the foods mentioned herein as being an asset in companies' ability to profit while simultaneously enhancing the well-being, personal growth, and self-empowerment of the worker, as well as corporate social responsibility, community service, and supporting a sustainable environment.

These companies include IBM, Google, AOL, Apple, Aetna, and Oprah Winfrey's Harpo Productions, Inc. **Meditation is one of the prime tools in the business setting to enhance the health, well-being, and productivity of employees, and aids in concentration, stress reduction, and creativity.** Some concrete steps that companies can take to feed workers "food that sustains life" is to:

- Engage consultants, professionals and experts in holistic modalities to facilitate classes, lectures, demonstrations, "Lunch and Learn" sessions, retreats, and individual or group coaching in various forms of meditation, psycho-spiritual mental health training, conflict management, and holistic fitness modalities such as Yoga, Tai Chi, Qi Gong, etc.
- Set aside time and space for employees to engage in individual and facilitated group meditation and dialectic sessions regarding workplace issues related to the company mission and individual roles and life purposes.
- Provide alternate holistic food choices in company-provided eating facilities.
- Encourage a safe atmosphere for employees to freely express and dialogue about their spiritual values, and
  - Promote activities that link employee personal gifts and life purpose with the company's mission.

CHAPTER 8

Summary and Review

Principal things to remember in incorporating a Soul-Over-Mind, DIS-EASE-is-the-cure approach to healing and problem solving.

FOREWORD, PREFACE, INTRODUCTION: <u>re-orienting your mindset regarding preventing, treating, and healing or resolving DIS-EASE challenges and symptoms you face or suffer from, as an individual, in relationships and organizations, and in the society at large.</u>

- **Start looking at disease, conflicts and problems as DIS-EASE**: spirit's attempt to heal the entity, a curative process manifesting as symptoms of distress or disruption within the organism or organism, whether it be that of the individual, relationships, the organization, the society, or the planet; psycho-socio pathology: to be cooperated with or augmented, not suppressed.
- **Be the Scientist**: When it comes to the prevention, treatment, and remediation of DIS-EASE in your sphere of influence, instead of depending slavishly on the opinions of so-called experts, validate them; also seek out alternative, complementary modalities; above all, take the best, leave the rest, and dare to perform your own experiments, i.e., take responsibility for your own well-being.
- **Be Prepared to "Lose Your Mind:"** stop depending solely on the mind to make important decisions. Seek spiritual in-

sight and sources of developing your intuition to help resolve issues that intellect alone is not equipped to resolve.

- **Be YourSELF**: recognize that the essence of you and others is not your person, your mind, your brain, your race, your religion, your nationality, your gender, your sexual preference, your material condition, your bank book, your intellect, your crazies, etc. Identify, first and foremost, with your (and others') soul essence, your immortal spirit, while at the same time acknowledging, respecting, and taking responsibility for the well-being of the various "suits of clothing" that you and others wear.

- **Make it Your Business to Incorporate Spirit in All You Do**: recognizing that, as important as career and material goals may be, the ultimate purpose of life is to realize your divinity and tap into it for success in everything you do, with ethics and integrity.

CHAPTER 1 - Embracing DIS-EASE As "Medicine," An Organism's Attempt to Heal Itself

- **The imperialistic mindset and approach to healing is a signature of largely western world national and political orientation based on the core theories of positivism and reductionism.** They reject the metaphysical and overly depend on simple physical laws to explain all intrinsic processes, the "war on cancer" being a perfect example of an imperialistic Mind-Over-Soul approach to healing versus treating DIS-EASE as the spirit's attempt to heal the body, which should be managed and cooperated with.

- **Cooperate with, rather than suppress, the organism's spirit-attempt to heal it.** Even when "emergency" or conventional intervention is necessary, incorporate long-term use of alternative modalities and lifestyle factors to prevent, replace, or complement suppressive treatment of DIS-EASE conditions.

- **Recognize the role of toxic or "enervating" ways of living and functioning as related to the root cause or prominent factor in the perpetuation of DIS-EASE,** rather than imperialistically going to war on or trying to "beat" the "disease" and "germs" (or people), as if they are the enemy to be suppressed, when in reality they are present in enervated organisms and play a role in forcing the alleviation of DIS-EASED conditions.

- **Dare to research, study, and experiment with alterative modalities**, like homeopathy, which, like the theory of toxemia, considers the totality of your symptoms: physical, emotional, mental, and spiritual.
- **Accept that in the process of holistically treating DIS-EASE, you may experience an aggravation of symptoms as you detoxify.** So, learn how to recognize the diminishing duration, frequency, and intensity, of recurring symptoms, and an increase in overall vitality as it proceeds in the direction of cure, and learn ways of easing the discomfort of detoxification as you persevere and the stay the course.
- **In the treatment of DIS-EASE, even if you need to incorporate some judicious use of short-term first aid, surgery, or suppressive drugs, the organism works to cure itself to the extent possible.** It does so if the patient pays attention to and cooperates with the organism's attempt to heal itself and provides food that nourishes and sustains life for the total body, mind, and spiritual needs of the organism.

CHAPTER 2 - Recognize the Power Within You to Create Your Reality by the Law of Attraction

- **Recognize that the body you inherit, and the life conditions you are born into is the "hand you are dealt," irrespective of your theories about epigenetics, karma, or the "sins of the father,"** and as such, by law, are the fruits of seeds sown. So, it's up to you to first accept what is, and decide what thought, word, and deed seeds to sow going forward, as you can and should influence the environment in which you live, and the lifestyle factors you adopt.
- **Remember, going forward, that every thought, word and deed you sow bears fruit and has a direct effect on you, your environment, and the people and things that occupy your mind.** So, plant only those seed thoughts that would manifest the highest ideals for which you strive, lest the projection of negative thoughts to others (and self) boomerang back on you.
- **Know that your ability to feel in the moment how it would feel as if the goal is already achieved is a magnet that can**

deliver it to you. So, when sowing seed goals, act like a person who actually expects the goals to manifest. However,

- o *****Remember that all efforts to use the law of attraction are subject to the natural and divine laws at work.** So, be wise and seek Higher Wisdom or divine guidance in choosing what goals to manifest, knowing that God or a Higher Intelligence already knows what is in your heart, and consider the truth as is stated in Biblical scriptures, "… seek ye first the kingdom of God, and his righteousness; and all these things shall be added unto you" (Matthew 6:28-33 - KJV).

CHAPTER 3 - <u>Analytical Trilogy and Recognizing the Relationship Between the Conditions You Experience and the Content of Your Inner Life</u>

- **Learn to conscientize** - be conscious of, rather than suppress, deny, distort, or overlook the truth of your reactions/habits/ errors, emotions, and thoughts, as truthfulness and consciousness is healing. Only suppression or indulging promotes DIS-EASE.
- **Remember that pathological symptoms, in self and in society, have a psychosomatic dimension.** The suppression of truth and consciousness leads to psycho-somatic conditions, i.e., those brought on by the emotional, mental state, and attitudes of a person.
- **Recognize when self and others are inverting reality.** Seeing good as evil and evil as good; believing that reality, not fantasy, causes suffering; seeing work as a sacrifice and laziness as pleasurable; thinking that love brings suffering and pain; and making wealth, prestige, and power the most important goals of all.
- **Recognize the dangers of inconscientization and envy:** the willful attitude of concealing, repressing, or denying one's consciousness. Hiding from oneself something one does not

wish to see, a psychological blind and unconscious wish to destroy the goodness and beauty we see in others and ourselves.

- **Recognize theomania, when ego acts as if it is infallible**, endangering the person who then has to bear the heavy burden of being the god-like creatures we think we are, thereby creating our own torture chamber as we struggle against our own nature.
- **Beware of demonic forces acting through self and others, in an attempt to alienate human beings from their true essence and divine calling and prevent them from realizing their divinity**. Recognize when we are possessed with the following: anger, ego, lust, greed, or attachment; addictions of one kind or another, causing us to overeat, lie, cheat, steal, get depressed or smoke cigarettes, drink alcohol to excess or use illicit drugs, or anti-social, addictive, or psycho-socio, pathological behavior, within self, in relationships, in society, and the world.
- **Commit to conscientization and interiorization.** Perceiving the existence of an inner psychological universe greater than our external universe and a return to one's inner self, to the source of life and happiness.
- **Beware of projection**. Recognize that what unduly or perpetually upsets you about the behaviors of others, or what you obsessively blame on others (projective identification) is a mirror bringing consciousness to you about yourself, and what you habitually fantasize about others (projective idealization) is an inflated image of them and a reflection of illusions you have about yourself.
- **Be sure to include aesthetic art and music in your life,** recognizing that it promotes inner equilibrium, nurtures the body and the emotions as well as positive thoughts, and aids in a conscious effort to do good in thought, word, and deed.
- **Remember that it is our prolonged reaction to "stressors," not the stressors themselves, that produces stress related afflictions**, manifesting as fear in predominantly depressive

individuals who may attempt to escape in usually passive, inactive ways, and as anger in predominantly paranoid-type individuals who react by attacking, hating, or fighting.

- **Commit to honestly assessing your own life to determine whether you are living too much in fantasy or escaping from an accurate perception of yourself,** escaping by over-indulging in an array of distractions, which may include: excessive reading, TV, social media, travel, addiction, over-eating, chasing sex, money, and social status, etc. (signs of prolonged inconscientized reactions to stressors).

- **Remember that being truthful or honest enhances one's ability to know the absolute truth,** a testimony to the power of the age-old axioms, "To thine own self be true" and, "Know the truth and the truth shall set you free."

CHAPTER 4 - Understanding the Scientific, Cosmological Process of DIS-EASE Creation and the Source of First-hand Spiritual Experience for Healing and Problem Solving.

- **In the process of incarnating and then ascending, human beings experience various planes of existence and an array of bodies that are related to these planes.** The onset of DIS-EASE mirrors this progression of creation, from idea to material manifestation. However, a Soul-Over-Mind, healing-through-consciousness orientation can reverse this process, leading to remediation, problem resolution, spiritual ascension, or reduced suffering.

- **There is an underlying unity of the various religious and spiritual orientations,** the ultimate goal of which is Self-realization and God-realization, or the union with the Supreme Being, and the Science of the Soul teaches how it can be achieved.

- **Mystics are saints or sages who have dedicated their lives to first-hand experience of the Beyond, and who have shared their experiences via various scriptures, writings, and the oral tradition.** They have existed in all the world's great religions, but mysticism itself is not a religion.

- **The mystic is concerned with those souls who yearn for a personal relationship with the divine so that they can find peace and harmony inside of themselves.** They urge seekers to perform their own experiments in order to realize the truth and apply it to their everyday lives and well-being by penetrating to the universal principles underlying their spiritual or faith tradition and practice.
- **Human beings often suffer a Mind-Over-Soul theomania with their ego envying God, seeing it as being Godlike.** Through it, the human being can be creative in the sense of thinking of something, especially material things, and attracting it into our lives, but cannot create a blade of grass, a grain of sand, or an immortal spirit.
- **A common theme running through most spiritual teachings is that the main cause of human problems is this attachment to the material side of life and a profound lack of knowledge of SELF whose essence is divine.** The root of the DIS-EASEs of humankind is a disconnection with the life-giving part of our being.
- **The Science of the Soul teaches that when we are able to raise our awareness beyond body/mind consciousness, we can avail ourselves of what they call "divine revelations,"** which serve as nourishment for the soul and a source of healing. The revelations convey divine wisdom to the soul and enlighten it to receive direct guidance from God, gradually replacing the limited decisions on the level of the human mind. These divine revelations reveal themselves to humanity in the form of inner light, sound "celestial music") and *Soma* (bliss).
- **Mystics consider divine revelations to be manifestations of what many religions call the "Word" or "Holy Spirit,"** an emanation from the Supreme Being that is a medicament for all ills, including bodily ailments like disease, sickness, old age; mental ills, like anger, ego, lust, greed, and attachment; and natural disasters.
- **When a human being does not realize who he/she is, in es-**

sence—an immortal divine spirit, not the mortal material body—one is susceptible to be ruled and manipulated by the ego/mind and material desires. This precipitates DIS-EASE in one form or another. However, obstacles and challenges are guideposts to our true purpose in the world. They are stepping-stones to genuine transformation for each of us as individuals, and through us, for humanity as a whole.

- **Evil, for the saint or sage, is anything that veers you away or limits you from striving toward union with the divine,** because the ultimate purpose of life is to realize your divinity. However, the evil forces don't want to lose control of one soul, even if it means entrapping the soul in the gold chains of fame and fortune or the iron chains of obscurity, discredit, and destitution.

- **In the process of human beings creatively manifesting results in their lives by positive thinking and the law of attraction, physical manifestation takes place in a certain sequence of Creation.** Ideas at the root of physical conditions are like software on thumb drives in a computer. They can be useful and nourishing or infected with viruses. In either case, DIS-EASE is designed to make us conscious of the underlying emotional, mental and idea patterns at the root of the conditions that we are suppressing, denying, distorting, or overlooking.

- **These DIS-EASE-producing ideas that nest within us can be seeded willfully or unintentionally by negative or demonic spirits.** The very process of conscientizing (neither suppressing nor indulging) symptoms, on the physical, emotional, mental, and idea level of our being, is curative and frees the life-giving spiritual energy to be redirected to wisdom, healing, and problem solving, by opening us up to divine inspiration.

CHAPTER 5 - How to Ignite the Healing of Dis-ease through Soul Therapy

- **A comprehensive Soul-Over-Mind approach to healing and problem resolution incorporates the "DIS-EASE-is-**

The-Cure" model of holistic health. This includes application of the law of attraction, the Science of Analytical Trilogy, and the cosmology of the Science of the Soul.

- **You can accelerate the healing of DIS-EASE by uprooting the underlying body/mind patterns at its roots.** These are patterns that have been suppressed, denied, distorted, or overlooked and that aid, abet, and have a causal relationship to the symptoms. To heal requires seeing and acknowledging the truth of these associations and our errors about them, rather than clinging to our inverted view of them.

- **To heal or remedy DIS-EASE, ultimately it is "the truth that sets you free," being committed to truthfulness or honesty in engaging in a dialectic with the therapist**. This normally opens one up to some higher wisdom and ideas, thoughts, emotions, and physical release associated with higher consciousness, because cosmologically, truth is synonymous with consciousness, love, spirit, and the Creator, all of which are eternal.

- **Understanding the relationship between cosmology and the process of creation helps the client to understand the root causes of DIS-EASE** and what it will take to contact the higher consciousness or message that the conditions are designed to bring to the client and thereby reduce suffering. As such, Soul Therapy provides tools that enable the client to use DIS-EASE conditions as medicine.

- **DIS-EASE symptoms are not, themselves, the root cause of the upsetting reactions, emotions and thoughts we have about them, nor are our parents, upbringing or relationships fundamentally to blame.** While others may have to pay for whatever wrongdoing or mistakes they make, and however true our assessment is of their behavior, the truth is that we attract people, environments, and experiences designed to bring consciousness to us and to develop us spiritually.

- **There's a tendency in people suffering from DIS-EASE to accept being victims and to blame (or project blame)**

99

onto others. For this reason, it is important to allow people to freely vent their reactions, feelings, and thoughts that they have. This tends to reveal how they project their own short-comings or fantasies, which is what really is at the root of the conditions they suffer.

- **We may have attracted certain behaviors of others to expose inherent conditioning within ourselves related to that behavior, as reflected in our genetics, karma, or the thoughts, words, and deeds we exercise via free will in this lifetime.** When clients acknowledge the truth of this, it makes it easier for them to forgive or persevere in spite of the misdeeds or evils of others, recognizing that one has within them the power to create their own destiny and need not wait to be liberated by others.

- **"Evil" is anything that turns the soul away from its inevitable reconnection to its Creator.** It doesn't matter whether one does good deeds or bad deeds, is charitable or miserly, is rich and famous or poor and infamous, it is evil if it limits one's connection to the source of creation and our life force.

- **It is the ego that doesn't want you to know your real identity as a divine soul with a higher purpose in life, destined to eventually reconnect in consciousness to the source.** This is because the ego is envious of the Supreme Creator, as ego can only attract things by thoughts, words, and deeds, but cannot create souls or energy; whereas it is the eternal Holy Spirit that pulls the human being's immortal soul towards the goodness, truth, and beauty of the Creator.

- **Suppressing truth or consciousness is tantamount to struggling against reality, against our own being, our real Self and our Creator.** Conversely, being conscious or truthful is embracing and reconnecting to our divinity. This opens us up to a taste of inner divine revelations that promotes enlightenment, wisdom, intuitive guidance, accelerated healing, problem resolution, reduced suffering, and heightened inner peace.

- **Soul Therapy is not a substitute for appropriate conventional medical or other professional consultation.** On the contrary, it is complementary to other healing and problem-solving modalities, and is deemed successful if it helps the client to experience the divine revelations and find additional necessary professional help, the energy to follow remedial regimens, and the will to progress spiritually and persevere in resolving chronic problems.

- **Successful immediate outcomes of Soul Therapy may include:** physically, a lighter feeling, as if a burden has been lifted, often including a measure of immediate relief of the presenting issues; emotionally, a calming down; mentally, more clarity of thought; causally, intuitive insights; and spiritually, a taste of peaceful joy or bliss.

- **Soul therapy is a deepening of the spiritual connection and preparation for advanced forms of higher healing and remediation,** i.e., self or God realization—experiencing one's divinity—which is the ultimate type of healing gained by higher forms of spiritual practice, especially meditation, under the guidance of those who have already reached or mastered that plateau.

- **The Soul Therapy formula is simple: being conscious is healing, whereas suppression of consciousness weakens our connection to our spirit, the source of life and healing,** and alienation from the spirit is tantamount to estrangement from its connection to its Supreme Creator, all of which is the root cause of DIS-EASE. This is true even if one intellectually believes in God. And this is as true for relationships, organizations, businesses, and societies as entities or organisms as it is for individuals.

CHAPTER 5 - Keys to Remedying DIS-EASE in Institutional and Relationship Settings Via Soul-Over-Mind Consciousness

- **Conflicts and obstacles are the soul of the entity's attempt to heal itself**. The act of facing and embracing obstacles rather than suppressing, denying, distorting, or overlooking them, releases the energy needed for resolution.

- **The pain and upset of conflicts and challenges in associa-**

tions makes us pay attention to what we may be ignoring. This enables entities to tap into an inexhaustible reservoir of inner resources to profitably work out relationships and do socially responsible business.

- **Associations, like individuals, are more than just its collective human minds or policies, procedures, goals, and objectives.** The lifeblood or essence of an association is that intangible asset within it, like the spark of divinity within the human being, that uses its "mind" and "body" (its human and structural facilities), and to which it must be continually re-connected, to resolve its DIS-EASE symptoms.

- **From a Soul-Over-Mind perspective, individuals within relationships and organizations can profit by employing consciousness and spirituality without compromising their personal religious beliefs.** As the essence of the word "religion" comes from the Latin root, "religare," i.e., re- (again, back) + ligare (to bind), it's the binding back again of the essence of the organism to its Creator source within it. Thus, within the entity itself, whether an individual or a group, is its own "house of worship."

- **To "cure" DIS-EASE in associations requires creating a safe space wherein associates can delve more deeply into the universal roots of their own religious, spiritual, or non-religious views of reality in relation to that of others.** Thus, firsthand experience of consciousness enables them to come together to discover the universal principles they share, rather than dwell on their differences.

- **At the root of DIS-EASE or conflicts in associations is role ambiguity, which exacerbates struggles between and among individuals to determine who makes the decisions to control and guide the use of shared space and resources.** Mediation of disputes or roles in organizations is a sort of collective attempt to meditate or concentrate on finding a unifying goal or objective to resolve issues that may have been ignored, suppressed, denied, or even swept under the rug.

- **Whether the "organism" is a human being, a relationship,**

or an organization, the root energy to heal it from conditions of DIS-EASE is found within it. This energy or life force is always working to evolve and grow the organism and does so with much less discomfort when we identify and cooperate with it.

- **Holistic food for an organization consists of its non-suppressive, nourishing high ideals and practices and socially responsible objectives and activities;** which, if employed, may require associations to work through temporary aggravation of symptoms to move in the direction of curing association ills.

- **Organizations can simulate the principles of Soul-Over-Mind through encouraging or supporting associates' individual efforts to meditate and explore alternative holistic practices.** This helps organizations to slow down and calm scattered, conflicting systems and interactions in order to access the "soul" of the organization and draw upon or reconnect to its "Higher Intelligence" and mission to facilitate healing and growth.

- **To avoid or resolve conflicts within organizations or relationships, the roles of individuals (their job descriptions) must align with the mission of the organization or relationship,** just as the periodic goals and objectives of workers in an organization or business must align with the current goals and objectives of the organization, all of which must be clearly defined, bought into, brought up-to-date, and made compatible with individuals' personal needs for fulfillment.

- **Role Mediation/Clarification should help workers (including management) become conscious of the congruency of organizational and personal missions, goals, and objectives in a way that they can realize the underlying unity to help ease conflict and achieve goals.** This process of Role Mediation/Clarification at the organizational level is epitomized by, and can be enhanced by, the process of meditation.

- **With a DIS-EASE-is-the-cure approach to healing, associ-**

ations, like individuals, benefit from consciously applying its will to discern what the organism needs and adopts an organizational diet, lifestyle, and culture or environment that, to the extent possible, nourishes and supports the organism. When we fail to properly nourish the organism or tune in to its innermost needs, it acts on its own to regain homeostasis. The result is perpetual or chronic conflict with attendant symptoms of pain and upset that make us pay attention to what we otherwise may have been too deaf, dumb, and blind to perceive.

- **Weaknesses in the original formation of an association "heredity," compounded by toxic environmental factors and a willfully unnatural or enervating work-life culture, overtaxes the organism's ability to eliminate its toxins and harmoniously carry on business.** When the organism is overwhelmed and blocked in its efforts to routinely eliminate toxic elements, it leads to an abnormal or heightened effort to detoxify, which the association experiences as conflict or DIS-EASE.

- **Long-term suppression of association DIS-EASE symptoms can evolve a condition from acute to chronic, wherein the association may still exist in a relatively pain-free, but illusionary, state of health.** But the organism will be in a much weaker state, operating at less than maximum capacity, its functions and major "organs" weakened, and vulnerable and susceptible to further, more chronic, or even degenerative DIS-EASE.

- **The ultimate object of facilitating the practice of meditation in the group setting is to temporarily still the organism's shifting, changing body/mind (its human and structural facilities), long enough to access its soul essence and Higher Intelligence.** In the process, one may intuitively access ideas and thoughts that can help resolve conflicts, meet needs, and enrich goal achievement.

- **In practice, meditation has documented innumerable benefits applicable to the lives of individuals at home, at**

play, and in organizational or relationship settings. This includes improvements in productivity, job satisfaction, and relationships; health and health habits; relaxation and decreased stress; memory, comprehension, creativity, perception, and the ability to focus and concentrate; self-actualization, intuition, and peace of mind.

- **Both Meditation and Role Mediation/Clarification in organizations begin with confronting (conscientizing) conflicting mindsets and altercations in the workplace**. In this context, the conflict or DIS-EASE is the cure. The organism's effort to expose and transcend obstacles that impede its effort to realize individuals and the association's "Higher Self," ideals, and "Higher Intelligence" or Mission.

CHAPTER 7 - Explains How to Enhance Healing through Soul-Over-Mind Modalities that Capture the Essential Life Energy, through Lifestyle, Diet and Energy-based Modalities

- **From a Soul-Over-Mind perspective, truly cultivating wellness requires us to nourish every dimension of our being, especially the Spirit.** In the face of DIS-EASE, it is imbibing the kinds of foods that sustain life and enhance prevention, treatment, accelerated healing, or remediation of DIS-EASE, rather than relying primarily on conventional means of suppressing symptoms.
- **What faith traditions call the "Holy Spirit" or "Naam" and various other labels in the different spiritual paths of the world, is the source of "divine revelations" as food or nourishment for the soul.** It is further channeled to human beings via the body's energy centers which absorb what is called "Chi" (Qi), or "Prana," the root food for the mortal energetic and physical bodies of human beings.
- **In the face of life-threatening DIS-EASES, those who best survive or thrive expand their notion of foods as: that which enables the human being to imbibe the actual "essential energy" that heals, prevents illness, and maintains wellness.** Three keys they employ are: 1) to consciously deepen their spiritual connection; 2) to see DIS-EASE as an opportunity to live life to the fullest, and not as a death sen-

tence; and 3) to incorporate alternative energy-based lifestyle and dietary measures as a permanent way of life, not just a temporary quick fix or silver bullet.

- **While there are all sorts of "experts" and professionals in each field, beware the ones who pressure you to limit your notion of DIS-EASE and foods to the conventional, that are so-called scientifically validated.** To best find out more about the energy-based foods, one is advised to be sure to research and enlist the aid of seasoned enlightened teachers who are skilled in their craft.

- **The supreme food of divine revelations as nourishment for the spirit is imbibed through the three pillars of the spiritual path:** *Silent Meditation* (beyond visualization) is a medicament for the health of the body, mind, and soul, and one hour of meditation can give as much relaxation as four hours of sleep; *Selfless service* is like a cash transaction—you get an immediate benefit of progress toward divine revelations—as you do with *Fellowship*—especially when it occurs in relationship with a saint or mystic.

- **The primary material sources of pranic food that sustain life consists of more holistic, natural elements, diets, and lifestyles.** This includes sunshine; oxygen (air); pure water; sleep and rest; live, plant-based natural foods; non-toxic personal care products; nutritional herbs, homeopathic remedies and whole food supplements; energy-based exercise; alternative consciousness-raising, energy-based healing modalities; fasting from toxic foods and other life elements that breed DIS-EASE symptoms; and cultivating higher forms of aesthetics and the arts: visual and performing. True art and aesthetics can expose pathology and enhance the connection for the human being between the physical, material world and transcendence. These foods act as a magnet in drawing out toxins and accelerating healing.

- **The movements of energy-based exercises stimulate healthy heart function and detoxification.** What many have in common is 1) making psychosomatic correspondences between DIS-EASE symptoms and ways of thinking and emoting; 2) providing maps of the body and ways to channel healing energy to related organs and structures; and 3) serving as complements to, and often substitutes for, conventional means of diagnostics and treatment.

- **Be brave enough to research, study, respect, and experiment with both conventional knowledge and alternative sources of expertise and mastery, based on ageless wisdom.** We live in a "how-to" culture in which often we look for "cookbook" methods to solve problems or attain success. And while it is true that in each field there are routine or even conventional things we may need to learn, what quickens and enhances this process is a Soul-Over-Mind approach wherein we first look to spirit for guidance and more intuitive ways to proceed and distinguish between conflicting claims as to efficacy.
- **Organizations, businesses, and associations would be wise to consider engaging consultants, professionals, and experts in holistic modalities** to facilitate classes, lectures, demonstrations, Lunch and Learn sessions, holistic food offerings, retreats, and individual or group coaching in various forms of meditation, psycho-spiritual mental health training, conflict management, and holistic fitness modalities such as Yoga, Tai Chi, Qi Gong, etc.

CHAPTER 9

DIS-EASE and Words of Wisdom from Practitioners

Examines experts' perspectives on DIS-EASE as a curative pro-
cess looking at so-called physical disease and other kinds of
extreme discomfort as a message and opportunity to rehabilitate
or grow spiritually.

Following are just a few of some special friends and colleagues who I've been blessed to know, and in some cases, be
treated by or collaborate with. In my view, they are some of the
known and unsung heroes and pioneers representing alternative
ways to view the world—ways that lay down a blueprint for the
healing of self and planet, of the body/mind and social DIS-EASE
that plagues us. Let us begin with an internationally-known giant
and national treasure born of the USA, Dr. George C. Fraser.

DR. GEORGE C. FRASER
www.onefrasernation.com

 Dr. George C. Fraser is Chair and CEO of FraserNet,
Inc., an award-winning 32-year-old global leadership
network of 91,000 black professionals, business owners, and community leaders. *Upscale Magazine* named
him one of the Top 50 power brokers in Black America.

As an entrepreneur and speaker, he focuses on improving
networking skills, building wealth, and improving diversity
and inclusion. Fraser has written nine books, including the

bestseller *Click*, spelling out the truths about the power of successful networking.

In 2011, Fraser was inducted into the Minority Business Hall of Fame and Museum. He has been awarded over 350 awards and citations from around the world, to include three honorary doctorates, a chaplaincy and an ambassadorship. He has put on the popular PowerNetworking Conference for the past fifteen years ... selected by *Forbes Magazine* in 2015 as one of "The Top 5 Conferences Not to be Missed by Entrepreneurs."

After 2019 he launched FraserNation, (www.onefrasernation. com), a "virtual nation" of "socially conscious" like-minded African descendent "Citizens," Citizen-Groups, Citizen-Organizations, and FraserNation allies banding together to build inter-generational wealth and develop new technologies for inter-connectedness and success in the 21st century.

Dr. Fraser shared that we are suffering the symptoms of DIS-EASE because, "...we are doing certain things outside of our comfort zone; the obstacle is put in our way to learn the lessons we need to learn to man up and women up to find a way around those obstacles."

Dr. Fraser quotes the Roman Emperor Marcus Aurelius, who said, "The impediment to action advances action. What stands in the way becomes the way."

Says Fraser, "The obstacle is the way; where there is no obstacle there is no way…it is purposely put in your way to find a way over or around it."

And when you successfully get past one obstacle, "God gives you a new assignment at another level … you remain stuck until you find a way over, around, or past it."

DR. AFRIQIYAH WOODS, PT, DPT
https://www.revolutionptnyc.com/

 Dr. Woods has over twenty years of experience practicing physical therapy in New York City, with expertise in treating orthopedic injuries, including treating professional and amateur athletes. She is also a certified clinical instructor for physical therapy students and family medicine residents at Mount Sinai Hospital. Afriqiyah has also served as a healthcare ambassador in East Africa offering physical therapy services and education to hundreds of rural patients.

Her doctoral degree is in physical therapy from Rosalind Franklin University.

For Dr. Woods, understanding that the DIS-EASE is the cure "may serve to get you out of your comfort zone to find your cure." Which means "you might have to be open to your unknown." For instance, some pains, like foot ailments may require you to, "step back out of the hectic rat race and look at some of the external and internal factors."

Sometimes a painful condition will cause a patient to have to look at their mindset and habits and see the relationship between their condition and certain material attachments, i.e., suffering from foot pains, "but wanting to keep shoes because of style or the fact that they bought so many of them."

Sometimes the dialectic between the practitioner and patient empowers them and is "more a key than the therapeutics ... so that when they are discharged, they recognize that it is important to continue with the tips I have given them and do the exercises on their own."

DR. ANTHONY SAEYGE
https://www.facebook.com/createdtothrive/

Dr. Saiyge is a holistic chiropractor based in White Plains, NY where he heads up the Thrive Holistic Healthcare organization. They utilize advanced computerized technology that can detect the hidden causes of any health problem with over thirty different techniques to correct the physical, chemical, and emotional blockages that can take place. What makes them different from most doctors is that they focus on correcting the cause instead of treating any symptoms or masking the problem. This allows the opportunity to get to a problem at its root and stop it from progressing.

According to Dr. Saeyge, the DIS-EASE is the cure, "If you address it." He says, "When I think of ease, I think of peace, everything flowing, things coming together naturally," because, "you're supposed to be healthy, prosperous, and successful." However, "When challenges come up in your life, it means using it as a process of getting where you need to go, of learning how to handle things better."

Dr. Sayegh says, ask yourself, "Is it important to just get rid of this pain? If you got the pain to go away, what would you do

110

about the problem?" (The DIS-EASE) "If your habit is to keep ignoring it, don't you need the symptom to kind of let you know that you need to be more loving and respectful of yourself?"

As soon as you recognize a lack of ease, stress, and tension building up, why wait until something fails? Your symptoms are your body's way of letting you know you've been ignoring this lack of ease for a little too long now ... you can sense it deep inside.

Address the cause of your symptoms. Know what your goal is, and ask yourself, "Where is my habit of thinking, and my actions based on that, choking out my ease, my peace, my sense of confidence?"

Why not, "Go ahead and allow a change from that divine spark inside and start allowing that inner wisdom to get you to start reflecting on the source of life inside."

DR. DERRICK TRENT
https://www.mindbodyshen.org/

 Dr. Derrick Trent is the founder of the Mind Body Shen System and the Mind Body Shen Network. He is a Grandmaster, Head Tai Chi instructor of MBS, a Qigong therapist, and a Recreational Consultant. Dr. Trent is certified by the NYC International Federation Division of Training, the Tai Chi International Federation, and the United Warrior Association. In addition to being a Tai Chi instructor, Grandmaster Trent has a doctorate degree in Chinese Medicine from Pacific College of Oriental Medicine, is a Board-certified, Licensed Acupuncturist, and holds a rank of 8th degree black belt with over thirty years of experience.

In the context of DIS-EASE is the Cure, Dr. Trent advises that, "The pain in the body is telling you that something is wrong. Address it. There's an imbalance." Modalities like Tai Chi are just a vehicle to help you fix the imbalance, to stimulate the organs to come into harmony with one another, i.e., the body begins to heal itself."

Dr. Trent gave fevers as an example, "It's a symptom not to just be suppressed or treated with drugs, because the drug doesn't treat the root of the problem, just the symptoms." For the doctor of Chinese medicine, the fever reveals something, "Now we can cure it; we know what to do to combat it."

At the core of Chinese medicine are psychosomatic (mind/body) correspondences to all the major organs, which practitioners classify according to five elements: **wood**-*anger*; **fire**-*joy;* **earth**-*sorrow*; **metal**-*grief;* and **water**-*fear*. This is critical to diagnosing and remedying the DIS-EASE. In order to understand the roots of DIS-EASE symptoms you suffer, to experience a remedy, not just a suppression, Dr. Trent advises you to do the work of researching alternative modalities such as Chinese Medicine, Tai Chi, Qigong, and Acupuncture.

DR. GEORGE LOVE, JR., DOM
http://bluedragonqigongacademy.com/

 Dr. Love, founder of Love Chinese Medicine, is a Florida-licensed primary care physician and certified Acupuncture Physician since 1986. He received his Qigong Master certification from Ju Shi Lin Taoist Scholars Council in 1994 and has been a teacher of Blue Dragon Qigong since 1983. Dr. Love is author of ten self-healing manuals, producer of multiple Medical Qigong videos and a radio talk show host for twenty years.

Regarding the idea that the DIS-EASE is the cure, Dr. Love immediately pointed to a simple thing like a fever: "Fever is the symptom created by the body to kill fungus, parasites, virus, bacteria; fever is the cure." He also links conditions to one's "emotional state: anger, frustration, shame, and guilt cause muscular contraction. The shape of the heart changes. Blood is not getting back into the heart." Literally, "broken heart" emotions restrict blood flowing into and out of the heart."

It is no wonder that "heart disease is the number one cause of death in the world. For Dr. Love, exercises like Qigong are an antidote to heart disease. "Qigong reshapes the heart and lungs … by training the blood to act in a certain way." The various movements of Qigong enable "muscles above, below, and around the heart to push blood into the different organs. Specific exercises will direct the flow back to its original normal state."

In addition to his prescription of Chinese Medicine, acupuncture, and Qigong, Dr. Love advises patients to "breathe, meditate, and relax to create normalization." And to do this, he says to have an "open mind. Cut your crap—your conditioned response and your negative responses to people trying to help you."

PETER LOPEZ, JR.
www.peterlopezjr.com

Peter is an international speaker, book publisher, and critically-acclaimed author. He's traveled all over the world consulting Fortune 500 companies like IBM, Google, Verizon, T-Mobile, EA Sports, Salem Communications, Wave Systems, Transamerica, and ING, and has spoken on the highest business, political, and spiritual platforms around the world. He has published 1,000 authors and currently represents five major publishing companies. His philanthropic work and humanitarian projects brought change to Cuba, Mexico, Venezuela, and thirteen other countries around the world. He specializes as a publishing guru, coach and consultant, social media advisor, and business developer.

In the face of DIS-EASE, Peter has experienced that "the uneasy feeling will become a cure" if you can find an inner calmness and peace and speak to yourself; master that factor." If in the middle of DIS-EASE, you become, "Self-aware and know who you are. It leads to an easiness to everything you do—not struggling anymore." You find yourself, "in a better place, physically, mentally and spiritually. It's a calming effect of where you are."

In the world of book publishing and writers, much of the DIS-EASE that Peter has seen manifests as, "Insecurity: Am I good enough? Who will read my story? Who believes in me? If I put myself out there, are the people going to buy it?"

When writers realize that it is a mindset that they can change, that, "what they call excuses and procrastination is insecurity, they can create a new blueprint of where they go next and be the architect of the design they have in your mind."

DR. CHARLES FINCH
http://www.charlessfinch.com/

Until June 30, 2007, Dr. Charles S. Finch III was Director of International Health at the Morehouse School of Medicine. He is a world-renowned Kemetologist ("Egyptologist") having conducted independent studies in African antiquities, comparative religion, anthropology, and ancient science since 1971. His work includes a collection of essays: The African Background to Medical Science, and the books, *Echoes of the Old Dark Land* and *The Star of Deep Beginnings: Genesis of African Science & Technology*.

As concerns DIS-EASE, Dr. Finch advised that, "All illness is a message to your spirit. This is one thing you learn in Africa. There is no cure in a traditional African sense, from the common cold to cancer and everything in between, unless there is a spiritual intervention. The spirit has to choose to cure you. If the spirit chooses not to, it isn't going to happen. And there might be all kinds of reasons for that."

There is a relationship between our thoughts, words, and deeds and the DIS-EASE that we suffer. "It's often the case that if you've done something that you weren't supposed to do, or there was an oversight or neglect. And it may be something that seems to have nothing to do with the problem at hand."

There is such a thing such as spiritual power that rules all things manifesting in different ways. And this does not just relate to a male God. I prefer the term Supreme Being ("Wa or Ua - the "One" in the language of Kemet - Ancient Egypt). It doesn't connote male or female. It's beyond life itself."

DOLORES WATSON
www.radianceretreatcenters.com

In the mid-1980s, Dolores founded Radiance, a holistic healing center in Harlem, NY, that transformed the lives of thousands of people through raw foods, juice fasting, purification, and meditation. She also founded the Radiance Retreat Center in Magnolia Mississippi, which today hosts a variety of holistic programs and retreats. Dolores's studies have brought her close to many spiritual traditions: i.e., born-again Christianity, the yoga and meditation practices of Hinduism, Vodou in Haiti, and, eventually in 2002, a commitment to Buddhism.

In the context of DIS-EASE is the cure, she says, "Discomfort is the path to seeking change in oneself, one's community, and the world. The discomfort, unhappiness, dissatisfaction, the abundance of desires and wants, all of these things were causing me to suffer."

It was Buddhism that made her come to this realization, in spite of a very successful career as a healing practitioner and entrepreneur. She shares, "Buddhism's main tenet is that life is suffering. I distanced myself from it. When I first became acquainted with Buddhism, I didn't realize I was suffering. I was too ignorant to realize it."

"It was only when I began to meditate and see from an internal perspective—from a soul perspective—that I could connect with the fact that I was suffering, and so is everybody else."

She says that material affluence doesn't shield us from suffering. "It's more difficult to see when we have all these material things. That's the trap that a lot of westerners fall into because there is so much abundance available to us. We are blinded by materialism."

DIVA JONES
msdivajonesny@gmail.com

 For over twenty years, Ms. Jones has been an international opera singer/vocal performer of music that heals, a holistic health practitioner, and a teaching chef. She has performed in the U.S, the Middle East, and all over Europe, including a command performance for the British Royal Family. A graduate of the Curtis Institute of Music, Ms. Jones has also worked as a teaching chef with opportunity youths, teaching healthy eating and social skills, and as an organizer of meals for the blind and elderly.

"DIS-EASE put my life on a whole new path. All I wanted to do was go around the world and be an opera singer. But then I got sick with sarcoidosis, a supposedly incurable, degenerative disease. The wisdom that I have gained from the sickness has been stunning."

Today Ms. Jones is almost fully in remission. She said, "I'm a walking miracle. A lot of goodness came out of the DIS-EASE in my life. It gets you in touch with life, and I am grateful that I have a life, because there were many times I thought I was leaving."

She said that you have to, "believe that it can change, and because something is in front of our eyes does not mean it's the truth. It's an appearance. When you are going through it, all you are trying to do is get to homeostasis. I was searching for peace in all of that." Above all, she said, "You have to have faith in God

115

to deal with DIS-EASE."

What really helped was "meditation every day, which was the most consistent thing in my life." And even though at times she was angry at God, "something also showed up giving me a glimmer of hope." She accepted that, "This is where I was supposed to be."

It took years of Ms. Jones working on herself, employing a host of holistic cleansing and detoxification modalities. Her recovery has given her the opportunity to "give back with whatever talents I've been blessed with … to live a life of upliftment … and bring other people to the healing work." Her voice is as strong as ever, and her vision is to share it wherever there is a need for healing and upliftment.

DR. KAMAU KOKAYI
www.healinghealthservices.com

Dr. Kamau Kokayi, M.D. is a world-class leading physician and the founder of Healing Health Services. He has been practicing for over thirty years and is a pioneer in the field of holistic, integrative medicine. Besides being trained and aware of the best in western medicine, he is foremost an expert in various non-allopathic (or non-mainstream) medical disciplines, including acupuncture, Chinese herbal medicine and theory, homeopathy, applied kinesiology, and a number of bioenergetic therapies.

As far as DIS-EASE is concerned, he says, "Illness can be a big part of our journey, depending on what we need to experience to manifest our highest expression." Sometimes it is the spiritual dimension that is calling out to us. "Universal Consciousness guides us back to this through blessings and lessons, but always helping us to move toward our highest calling: to be unique expressions of the divine." The ultimate solution? "Allow your full, spiritual, timeless self to be the one that is running the show."

CLAUDIA PACHECO, Ph.D.
www.stopradio.com

 Dr. Cláudia Bernhardt de Souza Pacheco, a psychoanalyst and writer for over thirty years has, since 1976, been Vice- President of the International Society for Analytical Trilogy, founded by Brazilian social scientist Dr. Norberto Keppe. She is also founder and president of the International Stop the Destruction of the World Association.

In response to the notion of DIS-EASE is the cure, Dr. Pacheco says, "In our work of integral psychoanalysis or Analytical trilogy, we see the symptom as an attempt to restore the inner balance of the organism that has been broken because of some attitude against our essence … we are creating disease in us.

"But what is at the root of this? A very dangerous attitude—censoring, repressing—concealing consciousness of what is wrong with us, as if we are perfect divine beings. We block energy that we need for a fluent process of healing, coming from consciousness, that can restore an inner balance … not just physical, but mental, spiritual, and socio-economic."

The source of this energy? "Essential energy comes to us through consciousness, that we can participate in God's infinite knowledge. To restore, we need a tolerance and openness to accept consciousness every time."

HASAN BAKR
www.hasanbakr786.com

 A master percussionist, singer, and composer having studied with a variety of music masters and performed with a number of artists at venues from Lincoln Center for The Performing Arts, to the Brooklyn, Academy of Music, to the Carnegie Hall Educational Series and elsewhere, nationally and internationally.

For brother Hasan, music plays a great role in healing. Sometimes in DIS-EASE, he says, "Success comes with being challenged. There are no setbacks. You will not find true success until you let go of the ongoing pursuit for convenience, the hunt for everything to be so easy. Judgement takes you

out of the brilliance of the moment."

"It is the step-by-step, finely applied basics that flowers genius or the fruits of your struggle in the moment—putting in a lot more effort. The people who sound like they are brilliant arduously apply themselves to the craft."

NOTE: Listening to this brother play the drums and other divine instruments one is reminded of what the saints call the "celestial music," the "Music of the Spheres," or the "Sound Current." This is the "music" one hears in higher states of meditation, and may manifest in the form of drums, flutes, etc., which are the source of the instrumental sounds in mundane music, and which, according to some saints, both purify the soul and keep the soul on the narrow path to Self and God-Realization.

BIBA PEDRON
https://www.bibapedron.com/en/meet-biba/

 Biba Pedron is an award-winning business coach, marketing expert, author, bestseller, and speaker known as the "Connection Queen." She is recognized as one of the Top Women Business Coaches in France and also works now in the USA and wherever called for. She has been honored by top female executives, professionals and entrepreneurs, recognized for Excellence in Business Coaching by Worldwide Who's Who, and named "Outstanding Entrepreneur of the Year" by The International Society of Business Leaders.

Entrepreneur Biba Pedron sees the business-related obstacles and challenges of DIS-EASE as being, "like a puzzle." And as a coach and mentor, she helps them, "put all the pieces together." She says that the wholeness is there to see if you know what to look for. Transformation is her main business product, which begins with, "Change the mindset first."

This, she says, helps would-be and current business owners to, "solve their problems, grow their businesses, and progress much faster than normal." Biba stresses that, "You can start your business on your own, but you can't grow it on your own; you will need help. Value the expertise."

DR. SERENA GOLDSTEIN, ND
https://www.drserenagoldstein.com/

Serena Goldstein is a NYC-based naturopathic doctor specializing in treating hormone concerns. She deals with issues surrounding weight, sleep, low energy, stress, PMS, peri/menopause, and andropause through nutrition, homeopathy, and botanical medicine and creates plans specific to each patient. She earned her Bachelor's in Psychology and Biology from Arizona State University, and her naturopathic doctor certification from the National University of Natural Medicine. Serena has been published in well-known health and wellness resources such as Consumer Health Digest and The Hearty Soul, and has appeared on Sirius XM, NYU Doctor Radio, and the Everlast Podcast (https://www.mindbodygreen.com/wc/dr-serena-goldstein).

For Dr. Goldstein, DIS-EASE, "is like peeling the layers off the onion, to balance us and piece us back together, uncovering more things as we heal. We have the possibility to be greater and heal on a far greater level than thought possible. Above all, Dr. Goldstein advises that, "health is so much more than our physical body; we need to start looking at spiritual causes of disease."

You can eat all the veggies, take all the supplements, and live the healthiest lifestyle possible, but still be unable to love self and others. It's a full time job, and when the switch finally flips in our brain, ego aside, we admit that we need help, enlist people on your team that you truly trust. Fortunately, there are many tools available in the toolbox. Use a variety of modalities. All that matters is what is here now; the path will provide us with the information we need. It is what brought you here."

JUDGE BENSONETTA TIPTON LANE
https://ballotpedia.org/Bensonetta_Tipton_Lane

Up until 2016, Bensonetta Tipton Lane was a judge of the 5th Superior Court District of Georgia. She was known as a fierce defender of civil and human rights, which wasn't always a popular posture to take. In 2014, she received a Legacy Award to honor judges who have exemplary records of judicial and public service and a commitment to innovative legal and judicial programs.

She received a J.D. from the University of Virginia School of Law, and over the years served on the boards of, or participated in, several progressive associations, including: Atlanta Volunteer Lawyer Foundation; Georgia Association of Black Women Attorneys (Co-founder); Metro Fair Housing, Inc.; Centennial Just Project (Founder); Alternate Life Paths Program; Sisterlove; and the Atlanta Chapter of the National Conference of Black Lawyers (Founder).

Many of the accused faced DIS-EASE symptoms early on that, if dealt with in the beginning or taken into account in sentencing, might reveal aggravating mitigating circumstances. The "healer" in this context is what is called the Drug Court or the Therapeutic Court. As such, Judge Tipton Lane addressed DIS-EASE in the context of the legal system, especially regarding defendants facing the death penalty, but also in a way applicable to less punitive sentences.

She says that the Therapeutic Court looks at the behavior complex (the DIS-EASE, of sorts) not just as symptoms to suppress, but as issues which represent mitigating or shaping factors that, if addressed, actually paint a picture of the most appropriate remedy or sentence. **The focus in the Therapeutic Court, based on what is called social or restorative justice, is on healing, which goes beyond the rush to punishment or the normal court procedures.**

Says the Judge, "In a death penalty case, the law requires a mitigation expert." The expert constructs a "Genogram," which, "follows every aspect of life. The mitigation reports are always heart-wrenching." They describe kids about whom, "No one did anything or cared," and wind up involved in, "…. drugs, streets, and then a killing."

Judge Tipton says, "It was there to see all the time. Neighbors and school saw … the broken education system … the middle-class guy stealing radios out of cars … burglary as a symptom of a drug problem." The therapeutic courts reveal that the symptoms could have been seen in the "original misdemeanors— the loitering, the drugs, or alcohol problem." If you are looking at, not ignoring or suppressing, the symptoms, you can see that they are, "growing like weeds." That is, until the DIS-EASE becomes degenerative. In this case, the death penalty.

DR. LAURI GROSSMAN
http://drlaurigrossman.com/

 Lauri Grossman is a licensed chiropractor and homeopath. A graduate of Cornell University and Hahnemann College of Homeopathy, she also serves as Chair of the Department of International Affairs at the American Medical College of Homeopathy and is a frequent lecturer there. Dr. Grossman has also taught at Memorial Sloan Kettering Cancer Center, the Hospital for Special Surgery, Lenox Hill Hospital, and Columbia Presbyterian Hospital. She developed the curriculum in homeopathy for the graduate nursing programs at New York University and the College of New Rochelle. Since the fall of the World Trade Towers, Dr. Grossman has served in numerous countries affected by natural disasters. Committed to improving the standard of health around the world, she has trained scores of physicians and nurses from developing nations in the use of homeopathic medicines for some of their countries' most pressing concerns.

When asked what the concept of the DIS-EASE-is-the-Cure means to her, in relation to her profession as a homeopath, Dr. Grossman advised that, "Homeopaths look at the symptoms as a guide to the thing in nature that will heal the person. The homeopath only uses the symptom as a guide as to what to prescribe." Regarding the importance of the intake process in homeopathy, Dr. Grossman stressed that, "They look at what makes each person's symptoms individual and unique ... and the healing can start before taking the remedy."

As in other holistic modalities wherein the organism heals itself, "Homeopathy stimulates the body to heal the symptom on the deepest level," and, "brings about a deep shift and global change—physically, mentally and emotionally. When the patient takes a potentized form of the remedy, their immune system responds in such a way as to halt the symptoms."

Dr. SHYA K. BEY
www.arise2it.com; www.docshya.com

 Dr. Bey is a Wellness activist and practitioner dedicated to getting the theory and practice of holism and "wellness wealth" included in the nation's health care system and all sectors of society. In preparation she has a broad educational background in wellness studies, spirituality, finance, engineering, and holistic modalities.

She has earned PhDs in Wisdom Traditions, Meta-Psychology and Music as a Reconnection to the divine, as well as an MBA specializing in small entrepreneurial businesses. And she is a non-denominational Ordained Minister. In addition, Dr. Shya completed four years in mechanical engineering after which she earned a post graduate certificate and insurance license from the New York Institute of Finance, qualifying her to work as a financial strategist with Series 6, 7 and 63 certifications qualifying her to trade stocks. Throughout the years Dr. Bey has capped off her learning with training in herbalism, Qigong and mastery in Tai Chi, and Reiki—a healing technique activating the natural healing processes of the body to enhance physical and emotional well-being.

Regarding the concept of DIS-EASE as cure she stressed that "to fix your lack of ease," on whatever level you experience it, requires you to understand that "the System is self-correcting and self-healing, and cure can only come internally; however, we must hear and respond to it to discover why we are not at ease."

She teaches that, "Like nature, our natural state is wellness—to be at ease." And Holistic wellness wealth Practitioners understand that, "None of us cure anything; all we can do is catalyze and support nature, and give the client the tools to activate what is already in them that is built in the system...The soul is the controller that runs the show....Eventually you have to acknowledge that its running without your assistance...You (the soul) are control but you (the person) are not in control."

So, "Minding your business is about *Life work balance;* your business should be minded by your real mind–your whole soul force—which is what holistic wellness wealth is all about.

AFTERWORD

Author's Summary Conclusions: WE DON'T HAVE TO SUFFER SO MUCH

Examines lessons and insights gleaned by the author and suggestions for how to take advantage of the information shared in this book.

If we only realized that there are precious jewels hidden in the DIS-EASE symptoms we suffer, then we would understand why the saints or mystics and spiritual masters say we should appreciate them, i.e., bear with them, rather than bemoan, suppress, or try to escape from the consciousness and actual healing they are trying to bring to us, because the DIS-EASE represents a debt paid and a highway to realization, if we would only seek spiritual guidance in being able to tap into the spirit to heal the DIS-EASE and reduce suffering.

This requires having enough humility to distinguish between "religion" practiced by the thousands of sects of various organized religions (and the multitude of 'isms' in all sectors of society), and universal consciousness—a process of self-mastery wherein we enter into our personal "house of worship" inside of us to reconnect with the life source of our creation, which is what all enlightened saviors and redeemers, after whom conventional religions are named, have implored us to do.

Even agnostics and atheists should be able to embrace spirituality in this sense. And finally, **let us recognize that our business in this life is not just our career goals, profit-making endeav-**

ors, or our material comforts, that making spiritual wealth and development a priority can do it all in the process bringing about a profound sense of fulfillment, inner peace, and freedom from suffering. That is, if we realize that we ARE suffering.

The Prison House of the Soul

I've had my share of suffering in the sense of my material existence. Most of us have, even the rich and the famous. However, there are peoples around the world suffering far more pain in the form of hunger, oppression, poverty, and sickness in a way that we in the USA can only imagine. However, in becoming a Soul Therapist, holistic educator, and seeker on the spiritual path, I have learned what suffering really means from a higher point of view.

Mystics teach us that it is the soul that is suffering, whether we are rich or poor, famous or obscure. The soul is trapped in this physical body without the opportunity to visit or go and come from its home, its birthplace in the higher spiritual realms. Saints know that there is a reason for the soul being here, that it has responsibilities to fulfill, and that it has to chip away the covering on it, like paint on a light bulb, in order to fully shine its light.

The happiness we experience is temporary. Fulfilling our worldly desires somehow leaves us still wanting. One spiritual student suspected that there was more to life than fame, wealth, pain, or poverty. And he began to feel that if somehow, we could consciously connect to our Creator and learn what he was sent here to accomplish in his earthly existence, then maybe he could find happiness. **So, he asked the master, "How does one know that they are doing the will of the Lord?"**

The master answered. "It's not necessarily when you are happy. It's when you are at peace."

Even if sometimes we have to make decisions and take actions that we don't feel like doing, if it begets inner peace, it is a signal that we have made contact with the spirit—with the divine. And in doing so, even if we have to endure some DIS-EASE, our suffering is diminished, and we are able to persevere.

Suffering and Disease in Everyday Life

Suffering the pain of acute and chronic conditions of DIS-EASE in some area of life or another is something we all probably recognize.

Take your pick. How can we cope and recover better from the misery attendant with deaths, breakups, betrayal, love lost, divorce, problems at work, job loss, money loss, incarceration, public humiliation, stress, nagging health issues, or insecurities stemming from social unrest, crime, natural disasters, wars and conflicts?

What can we do to get more insight into how to resolve difficult encounters with the opposite sex, family, friends, co-workers, authority figures, bosses, subordinates, or workers? It helps to cultivate a better relationship with your self—not just your person, but your essential self, your spirit.

Know Thyself

Sages teach that reducing suffering, being at peace, and curing the DIS-EASE conditions in your life requires prioritizing the search for knowledge of self as a divine spirit and realizing its connection to your divinity as the source of your life and healing.

Christians know what I mean. There is something written in the Bible that we can all learn from, irrespective of our religious or spiritual affiliation or perspectives. Matthew 6:28-33 (KJV) says:

> **Sages teach that reducing suffering, being at peace, and curing the DIS-EASE conditions in your life requires prioritizing the search for knowledge of self as a divine spirit and realizing its connection to your divinity as the source of your life and healing.**

28 And why take ye thought for raiment? Consider the

lilies of the field, how they grow; they toil not, neither do they spin:

29 And yet I say unto you, that even Solomon in all his glory was not arrayed like one of these.

30 Wherefore, if God so clothe the grass of the field, which today is, and tomorrow is cast into the oven, shall he not much more clothe you, O ye of little faith?

31 Therefore take no thought, saying, What shall we eat? or, What shall we drink? or, Wherewithal shall we be clothed?,

32 (For after all these things do the Gentiles seek:) for your heavenly Father knoweth that ye have need of all these things.

33 **But seek ye first the kingdom of God, and his righteousness; and all these things shall be added unto you."**

And where is the "Kingdom"? It's not in the cozy bubble around you. It's inside of you.

Come out of Your Bubble

To come out of your bubble that imprisons your soul requires that you see the relationship between the suffering DIS-EASE conditions you face and the underlying mind/body patterns that you may be suppressing, denying, distorting, or overlooking.

So, what is YOUR bubble? Is it your race, your gender, your nationality, your caste or class, your profession, your circle of friends, your religion, your programmed family traditions and beliefs, your money, your good looks or flashy clothing, your empty pockets, your health limitations, your addictions, your handicaps, your genetics, or karma? **Or, could it really be, in essence, your mindset and the corresponding DIS-EASE conditions it attracts?** Whatever your answer, it is sure that it exacerbates the suffering you endure. Maybe you need to change your "diet."

Try Imbibing More of the "Foods" That Sustain Life, Starting with Your Spirituality

To endure and rise above suffering, you may have to explore nourishment outside of the bubble you normally reside in. It means becoming more the scientist of the soul, not just for or against the polemics and trappings of the religion you have been brought up in, but seeking first-hand, direct spiritual experience. It may also mean fasting from foods and ways of living that breed DIS-EASE, thus allowing the body to heal itself, or for the spirit in the body to heal it.

It means becoming more aware of the workings of all of the bodies worn by your soul and the planes of existence that they correspond to.

It means exploring a plethora (or variety) of different alternative therapeutic and restorative modalities to complement and broaden your current level of knowledge; and be more discriminating regarding the actual effectiveness of the modalities that you are aware of or that are impressed upon you.

It doesn't mean that you summarily forsake all of the pleasures and materials of life or become completely lacking in desire. So, why do some saints say, "A desireless man is no less than God"?

They simply advise that you raise your level of desire to the spiritual nectar that is more intoxicating, more lasting, and without the suffering of withdrawal symptoms attendant with the material desires we normally crave and indulge. *Your material desires are effects that mimic the yearning your soul has for consciously reconnecting with the divine, just as sure as a physical orgasm, delicious though it may be, pales in comparison to a taste of the honey of enlightenment.*

Dare to Profit by Consciousness of the Inner Causes of the DIS-EASE Symptoms You Face

It's time for a new paradigm, one in which we acknowledge, honor, and take advantage of the pre-eminence of consciousness and the healing spiritual life force operating in all sectors of

> **It's time for a new paradigm, one in which we acknowledge, honor, and take advantage of the pre-eminence of consciousness and the healing spiritual life force operating in all sectors of society and in the lives that we live.**

society and in the lives that we live.

This transcendent soul force is the true "self," or life blood, in all manifestation. And Sages advise, "To thine own self be true." Self-mastery means that the ego, which thinks its God-like, must be put in its proper place, as a good servant but a poor master. This will require you to open up to other lines of research in order to address and remedy the DIS-EASE issues that you suffer in all phases of your life. In your search, you can take the best and leave the rest. But simply going through the motions makes this more difficult.

From Ritual to the Real Thing

In every phase of life, we engage in rites, rituals and ceremonies to help take advantage of and become accustomed to the benefits they promise. **Many rituals may take us far in the direction we are headed. However, they are most profitable if they spur us to actually engage in the direct action that delivers the ultimate fruits that they promise.** The reader is urged to research their own scriptures or traditions for analogies to the examples cited in the following section in order to get beneath the surface to the universal meanings taught by the realized beings in those traditions and to appreciate similarities to other traditions.

Take, for example, the beautiful ritual of communion in Christendom. In the Bible, Jesus reportedly advised His disciples that, "Whoso eateth my flesh, and drinketh my blood, hath eternal life; and I will raise him up at the last day." (John 6:54 - KJV).

So, churches around the world practice the ritual of Communion, or the Eucharist, in which the congregation imbibes a cracker and wine, or juice, to symbolize imbibing the body and blood of Jesus in order to achieve eternal life.

Obviously, however, Jesus was not a cannibal. In His own words, the true identity of Jesus was not the body but the Holy Spirit; as the Bible says, "And the Word was made flesh, and dwelt among us, (and we beheld his glory, the glory as of the only begotten of the Father,) full of grace and truth." (John 1:14 - KJV)

So "the only begotten son" was the Holy Spirit, or "Word," manifesting in Jesus who advised His disciples to imbibe this "body and blood" in order to realize God. This Holy Spirit is manifest and realized in all true Saints, sages, mystics and enlightened beings, before, during and after the time of Jesus— including Moses, Mohammad, Krishna, the Buddha, Lao Tzu and, no doubt, in countless times and climes and others, unbeknown in the deep recesses of the developing areas of the world. **The Holy Spirit is in us too, but not yet realized.** However, if Communion, in and of itself, does not guarantee this realization, what does?

Jesus gives a clue. He advises, "God is Spirit, and those who worship Him must worship in spirit and truth." (John 4:24 - KJV)

Jesus is suggesting that the key is to enter into the Kingdom of God inside in order to reconnect with God the Supreme Being. Mystics teach that this is the true meaning of the ritual of "baptism", which enlightened spiritual masters call "initiation". In common religious ceremonies, dunking into the water symbolizes being bathed in the Holy Spirit. Saints say that the Holy Spirit manifests in man as inner light, sound and bliss—the Divine nectar that draws up the soul to union with the Divine. The key to moving from ritual to direct experience, they say, is meditation. Of course, it all depends on your goal as to what system you use. You can reap many material benefits of many methods which call themselves "meditation," but that focus mainly on concentration, which is a precursor to the higher forms of meditation employed by mystics. Enlightened Saints teach a form of silent meditation - for the seeker who wants to rise in consciousness beyond the regions of the mortal mind to ultimate union with the Divine, while still accruing the material benefits of concentration.

Meditation and Prayers

In one respect, prayer is like a beautiful ritual in preparation for the real thing, which is rising above body consciousness and actually experiencing the fruits longed for in supplication or prayer. Spiritual Masters teach that prayer is a way to give thanks for the grace and mercy of the Giver of life, to be grateful for all the blessings we have, to seek understanding to do the right thing, and to have the strength to be a better person and seek the wisdom and Divine will of the Creator.

Given the law of attraction, hopefully this leads to action: to direct experience in order to reap the fruits of what we long for in prayer. This is the divine purpose of meditation, to "be still and know that I am God." (Psalm 46:10 - KJV).

It is true that, for the average person, meditation takes practice. I'm often told how difficult it is to stop the mind from drifting all over the place. I say, "Duhh, that's why you meditate, to discover firsthand that you have little control over the mind, and that this is a prime source of the DIS-EASE we suffer."

One particular mystic, Soami Divyanand, suggested ways to deal with this. He calls it "Turyia," or Meditative sleep. Instead of going to sleep with the tv, radio or iPod on, lay down and focus on the Third eye, which is above and behind the eyebrows, and keep repeating Sacred names of the Divine (or what you consider the creative life force) until you fall asleep. He says that rather than experiencing dreams that regurgitate the thoughts, words and deeds of the day, Turyia leads to the experience of visions that help to spur your spiritual growth and insights. Furthermore, if you are fortunate enough to be able to sit a long time in meditation, seemingly at the expense of sleep, you still wake up refreshed in the morning. I can attest to this. It's like Saturday night at the movies.

Divyanand also suggests that you do this meditation exercise first thing in the morning for a few minutes to stamp the day's activities with some divine nectar. Also, during the day, take out five minutes at a time to "meditate" when having difficult decisions to make and when intellect alone doesn't suffice. Concentration leading to meditation wherein the awareness gets beyond thought leads to intuition and divine wisdom in conducting the affairs of life. The masters call this intuition "Divine Revelations," which Divyanand says are actually the "angels" who seekers yearn to come in contact with.

Divine Revelations

Mystics teach that Divine Revelations, accessed in higher states of meditation, disclose themselves in the form of inner light, sound ("Celestial Music") and bliss—inner peace; divine guidance, wisdom, and intuitive insight; enhanced energy and vitality; reduced suffering; and accelerated healing of body/mind, in self, relationships, institutions and society. While for some, this kind of ability is "hardwired," to an extent, in their genetic structure, it takes the guidance of one who has mastered the science and art of it to be able to manifest it at will.

Masters, Mastery and Self-Mastery

This is where "the rubber meets the road" in the discussion of Soul-Over-Mind. For some, the word "master" connotes "slave". Actually, I heard one master say that he is the "slave of the slave", meaning he is in surrender to the Holy Spirit which is the "slave" assigned to do the work of the Lord.

A true "master" (in any field) is not there to subjugate you, but to train you as an apprentice, help guide you to self-mastery and, in the process, reduce your suffering. "Yo momma" was your first master. Many of you report to your teacher as master who decides whether you get to receive that master's degree. The jet pilot is your master when you hop on that airplane and it takes off.

There are "masters" in every field of endeavor. Why not masters in the field of spirituality? It's true that there are also charlatans in every field of endeavor, including in the field of spirituality. So, how do you get around that? Mystics say that you earn the teachers you engage by virtue of your destiny—what you are ready for at a certain point in life in route to higher consciousness, as you plow through the DIS-EASES of living.

Are you already on the path or geared up for the journey to Self-Mastery and are open to the guidance of a true master? Not to worry about whether they exist or not, whether they are genuine or not, or whether you can actually achieve mastery. Truth be told, say the saints, TRUE MASTERS FIND YOU, not the other way around. In a great book called the "Kybalion", the "master of masters", Hermes Trismegistus, deified as "Thoth" (or "Tehuti" in Kemetic or Egyptian lexicon), uttered the following insightful words:

- "Where fall the footsteps of the Master, the ears of those ready for his Teaching open Wide."
- "When the ears of the student are ready to hear, then cometh lips to fill them with Wisdom."
- "Milk for babes, meat for strong men" ("meat" meaning sustenance, not the flesh of animals)

Your job is to answer that calling deep within your heart, pining for the Divine, to seek knowledge of self and be true to self. Regarding spiritual masters, some people even experience such guides inside, before or after coming face-to-face with them. In the long run, they say, you don't really *know* a master until you have that experience.

Many don't believe that it is possible for there to be enlightened beings other than the ascended Savior associated with their particular religion. My view is that such people may not actually believe that they, too, can realize *their own* divinity, while walking planet earth, not waiting until they die and go to heaven. For Christians, Jesus underscores this point in speaking to the people standing in front of him, in that time and clime: "Verily, verily, I say unto you, He that believes on me, the works that I do shall he do also; and greater works than these shall he do; because I go unto my Father." (John 14:12 - KJV)

"Believing on me" is believing on the Holy Spirit; and, you don't necessarily have to wait for an ascended master or one embodied with the Holy Spirit to return. For me, I can't imagine that our Creator would ever leave His children alone, adrift and bereft of living guides to help us navigate the tumultuous DIS-EASES of life.

Furthermore, for me, I treasure mastership in any person, in any field I encounter where it helps me to prevent, treat or heal from DIS-EASE. I trust the latent desire in my heart to know God, and that it will lead me through whatever experiences I need to have to become realized. So, instead of summarily dismissing the possibility of living masters of spirituality as there are in every field, open your heart, study and be a magnet that attracts them. For me, the search for spiritual guidance is also a way of striving to see the "Christ," or Holy Spirit, in others.

Love and Forgiveness
Many throughout the ages have glibly ruminated or even sermonized about this thing called love. As master musician Bob Marley crooned, "Yah mon…one love." However, masters teach that this requires seeing God and spirit in self and others, which is easier said than done. We have all experienced those who say they love us, but what we feel from them is more like lust or conditioned love with all its strings attached.

It takes access to spiritual power or consciousness to love, and especially to forgive those who kick you in the butt. Some have done so—i.e., spiritually guided men and women like Dr. Martin Luther King, Harriet Tubman, Nelson Mandela, Mother Teresa, and countless other giants that you may be aware of in the cultural context in which you live.

The masters teach that the more you cultivate your spiritual nature, and gain access to Divine Revelations, the more love will power you, not the other way around; you will more likely be love. And this love is the spiritual source of healing. And what's in it for your spirit to lend its life force to heal you? Because as long as you have one breath left in your body, you have the opportunity for enlightenment—union of the soul with its Creator.

I've learned that if it's worth doing, it's worth doing it with affection, even if it's mopping the floor, or working on

a job you hate until you've learned the lesson it is trying to teach you to liberate yourself from the DIS-EASE of it. This is what I've dedicated my life to, and so have so many others with whom I have met and collaborated. We are dedicated to putting the science of spirit back into all dimensions of life and all sectors of society, to enrich life and remedy all manner of DIS-EASE.

Use us - the Practitioners Guided by the Spirit

We are the ones for whom work is a spiritual path. We respect whatever goodness there is in any healing modality but offer alternative approaches to complement or eventually supplant some of the conventional means at your disposal, especially when they are failing to get results. We are the ones who don't just want to quick-fix you but want you to become self-mastered. We are the ones who want to help you transform your DIS-EASE symptoms into guidelines for cure or remission. We are ones who want to help you elevate your mindset and let it be guided by spiritual consciousness or Soul-Over-Mind. We are the ones who understand how the DIS-EASE is the cure. And we are the ones who offer a better way to mind your business.

So, I urge you to treat the information in this book as a paradigm to see what of it that you, in your professional and personal wisdom, can apply to your life and field of endeavor. Please do look us up, engage our services, research what we are teaching; and see for yourself, because as the sage says, "seeing is believing". Hopefully this book has provided for you some knowledge, links, and identified resources to inspire you in your search.

Namaste (I salute God within you)
As-Salaam-Alaikum (Peace be unto you)
Shalom (peace)
Wu liang guang (heavenly blessings upon us)
Em hetep (in peace)

And to all other languages, peoples and faith traditions:
May God or the Oneness be with you

Leonard "Len" Burg

WEBSITE: www.InnerspireTherapeutics.com
EMAIL: Lburg@InnerspireTherapeutics.com
FACEBOOK: Facebook: /InnerspireITI
TWITTER: Twitter: @LenBurg_innersp
LINKEDIN: www.linkedin.com/in/lenburg
INSTAGRAM: www.instagram.com/lenburg_innerspire/

Endnotes

1 **NOTE: this quote represents the more enlightened Gandhi, not the young man living in South Africa who saw himself to be in a caste above the colored "kafirs", a pejorative label given black Africans. He was not, during his life, a perfect man, nor did he claim to be a saint. However, whatever good he did do was no doubt inspired by these words—the essence of which all of us can be guided by.

2 The Universal Tone, Carlos Santana, Little, Brown and Company, New York, NY USA, (2015 page 331-333)

3 Power vs. Force - The Hidden Determinations of Human Behavior, David R. Hawkins, Ph.D., Hayhouse, Inc., Carlsbad CA, USA (2012 page 313).

4 Power vs. Force - The Hidden Determinations of Human Behavior, David R. Hawkins, Ph.D., Hayhouse, Inc., Carlsbad CA, USA (2012 page 313).

5 Stolen Legacy, George G.M. James, CreateSpace Independent Publishing Platform, Amazon.com, (2013 page 7)

6 The Universal Tone, Carlos Santana, Little, Brown and Company, New York, NY USA, (2015 page 330)

7 https://www.simpletoremember.com/articles/a/einstein/

8 Power vs. Force - The Hidden Determinations of Human Behavior, David R. Hawkins, Ph.D., Hayhouse, Inc., Carlsbad CA, USA (2012 page 313).

9 The Universal Tone, Carlos Santana, Little, Brown and Company, New York, NY USA, (2015 page 329)

10 Toxemia Explained, John H. Tilden, M.D., Republished by David Klein, PhD., Online Book Store, (2010, loc. 176)

11 "… man is the crown of creation, and this spark was placed in him by the Creator of the Universe Himself" - From "Scholars Speak of God" Reprinted from Orthodox Life Vol. 44, No. 6 November - December, 1994 (see http://www.tcgalaska.com/holycrosshermitage/pages/Orthodox_Life/scholars.htm

[12] Toxemia Explained, John H. Tilden, M.D., Republished by David Klein, PhD., Online Book Store, (2010, loc. 509)

[13] *Ibid, location 1044*

[14] Organon of the Medical Art, Dr. Samuel Hahnemann, M.D., edited by Wenda Brewster O'Reilly, Ph.D., Birdcage Books, Palo Alto, CA USA, (1996, location 1948)

[15] Advanced Treatise in Herbology, Dr. Edward E. Shook, Trinity Center Press, Beaumont CA, (1978 page 109)

[16] https://www.oakpark.com/News/Articles/2-17-2009/Mozart-vs.-Salieri:-Genius-vs.-jealousy/

[17] Nature Versus Nurture, Saul McLeod, Simplypsychology.org, https://www.simplypsychology.org/naturevsnurture.html, (2018)

[18] https://www.etymonline.com/word/oracle

[19] The Crown of Life, Kirpal Singh, Ruhani Sat Sang, Blaine, Washington, (2012, pg. 30)

[20] https://www.brainyquote.com/quotes/napoleon_hill_392258

[21] The Secret, Rhonda Byrne, Atria Books, New York, NY USA, (2006, pages xi, 68 and 177)

[22] Resurrection, Neville, Devors & Company, Marina Del Rey, CA, (1990, pg. 10)

[23] *Ibid.* pg. 5

[24] *Ibid.* pg. **42-43**

[25] The Universal Tone, Carlos Santana, Little, Brown and Company, New York, NY USA, (2015 page 329)

[26] (https://www.amazon.com/Healing-Power-Water-Masaru-Emoto/dp/1401908772/ref=sr_1_3?keywords=The+Hidden+Messages+in+Water%2C&qid=1575592576&sr=8-3)

[27] The Secret Life of Plants, Peter Tompkins and Christopher Bird, HarperCollins, New York City, USA, (1973)

[28] Psychotherapy and Exorcism, Norberto Keppe PhD. Proton Editora Ltda., Sao Paulo Brazil, (2018, p.2)

[29] Healing through Consciousness; Theomania, the Cause of Stress, Claudia Bernhardhardt Pacheco, Proton Editors, Ltda., Sao Paulo Brazil, (1983, p. 138)

[30] Liberation of the People; The Pathology of Power, Norberto R, Keppe, Ph.D., Proton Publishing House, New York, NY USA, (1986 page 322)

[31] *Ibid, page 323*

[32] http://www.stopna.org/glossary-of-terms/, Stop the Destruction of the World Association North America top the Destruction of the World Association Brazil, Sao Paulo Brazil and New York USA

[33] *Ibid*

[34] *Ibid*

[35] A New Earth: Awakening to Your Life's Purpose, Eckhart Tolle, Penguin Books, London, England, (2005, p. 246-248)

[36] The Unquiet Dead - a Psychologist Treats Spirit Possession, Dr. Edith Fiore, Ballantine Books, New York, NY USA, (1988, page 194)

[37] *Ibid,* p. 19

[38] Psychotherapy and Exorcism, Norberto Keppe PhD. Proton Editora Ltda., Sao Paulo Brazil, (2018, pg. 19)

[39] *Ibid*

[40] Healing through Consciousness; Theomania, the Cause of Stress, Claudia Bernhardhardt Pacheco, Proton Editors, Ltda., Sao Paulo Brazil, (1983, p. 31)

[41] *Ibid, pg. 32*

[42] *Ibid*

[43] Kirpal Singh, Unity of Man Website, http://www.uom-conference.org/index.php/en/unity-of-man/sant-kirpal-singh, Unity of Man Website, 2019

[44] The Crown of Life, Kirpal Singh, Ruhani Sat Sang, Blaine, Washington USA, (2012, pg. 338)

[45] Stolen Legacy, George G.M. James, CreateSpace Independent Publishing Platform, Amazon.com, (2013 page 7)

[46] Beware of Sects, Soami Divyanand, Divyanand Verlags-GmbH, Herrischried West Germany (1989, pg. 83)

[47] *Ibid, pg. 82*

[48] THE ONE - Multiple Names of THE ONE that cannot be named, sneharani2005, Coursehero.com, https://www.coursehero.com/file/15184836/THE-ONE/

[49] Naam or Word - ISBN 978-0-942735-94-9, Kirpal Singh, Ruhani Satsang, Blaine, WA, USA, (2017, pg. 135)

[50] The Way: Using the Wisdom of Kabbalah for Spiritual Transformation and Fulfillment, Michael Berg, Wiley, Hoboken, NJ USA, (2002, page 23)

[51] "Anchoring in neuro-linguistic programming is a term used for the process

by which you apply a gesture, touch or sound at the peak of a state, either in oneself or someone else. The said anchored state can then be recalled or re-activated by reapplying the gesture, touch or sound."; https://www.nlpworld.co.uk/nlp-glossary/a/anchoring/

[52] You can Heal Your Life, Louise L. Hay, Hay House, Inc., Australia, (2004, page 6)

[53] Not everyone believes there is a God or what God is. Here we simply define God the oneness underlying your higher sacred self, a higher intelligence, a Supreme Being, The All, The Creator or the source of all creation.

[54] *Webster's Revised Unabridged, 1913 Edition; (Page: 58)An"i*mus (#), n.; pl. Animi (#). [L., mind.] Animating spirit;*

[55] "Relating to or causing disease; pathogenic"

[56] "NATUROPATHIC HEALTH CARE"; "The natural state of the human organism is health and homeostatic balance. The body can heal itself if not blocked. The task of the practitioner is to help bolster the patient's own healing capacity..

[57] In the book, "Zen and Creative Management", by Albert Low, the author describes how conflict arises in organizations when people, like animals, act to guard their "territory" or the space they occupy and attempt to control.

[58] The Tao of Leadership, John Heider, Humanics Limited, Atlanta Georgia, USA, (1988, page 115)

[59] Eastern Mystics call this process "God Realization"

[60] How to get chi energy?, http://wiki.answers.com/Q/How to get chi energy

[61] The Role of Prana as the Energy of Consciousness, Gopi Krishna, Institute for Consciousness Research - Kundalini & Consciousness Researh, http://goo.gl/Vwdum

[62] Meditation as Medication for the Soul, Rajinder Singh, Radiance Publishers. Kindle Edition. Lisle, Illinois, USA., (2013 location 97)

[63] From Fast Foods to Slow Foods - How to Wake up Laughing, Yvonne Stafford, Natural Living Press, New York, NY USA, (2011 page 76).

[64] Meditation as Medication for the Soul, Rajinder Singh, Radiance Publishers. Kindle Edition. Lisle, Illinois, USA., (2013 location 223)

[65] The Better Business Book, Volume 2, Tyler Wagner, Authors Unite, www.authorsunite.com, (2017 Page 307)

APPENDIX I

A Technique of Meditation

Meditation, in its essence and higher aspect, begins after, through concentration, all thought stops, and one becomes aware of the underlying reality of one's Higher Self (Spirit) and the infinite Higher Intelligence (God) with which it is connected.

In the Surat Shabd Yoga system of meditation[1], there are three main stages. For the ordinary person, without the benefit of guidance from a master of meditation, it is progress enough to approach the second stage—concentration—wherein all thought stops. Such persons who go beyond that point are likely to have come into this world predisposed to experience that level.

Meditation masters distinguish between efforts called meditation but are really "concentration" (which is a prerequisite for meditation). Such efforts may engage the five senses through verbal chants, breathing, counting of beads, candles, incense, etc. Beyond that, for the saints, is union with God in the spiritual realms beyond the mind—the ultimate goal of meditation. The following method is suitable for seekers who want to eventually go beyond concentration, with the goal of revealing God inside.

---

[1] "Surat Shabd Yoga"; *Wikipedia, the free encyclopedia (http://en.wikipedia. org/wiki/Surat_Shabd_Yoga). "*As a Sanskrit term, *surat* means "soul," *shabd* means "word" and *yoga* means "union." The term "word" means the "Sound Current," the "Audible Life Stream" or the "Essence of the Absolute Supreme Being," that is, the dynamic force of creative energy that was sent out, as sound vibration, from the Supreme Being into the abyss of space at the dawn of the universe's manifestation, and that is being sent forth, through the ages, framing all things that constitute and inhabit the universe.[1].

We may at first see either darkness or light, sparks of light, pinpoints of light, flashes of light, circles of light, or light of any color, such as red, orange, yellow, blue, green, purple, violet, white, or a golden color, or nothing at all. It differs at the outset according to person. Or we may see inner vistas such as an inner sky, clouds, stars, a moon, or a sun. Whatever, we should just continue gazing into the middle of what appears.

Stages of Meditation

1. *Repetition; remembrance*[2]: Here one withdraws attention from outside objects and concentrates it in the eye center, between and behind the eyebrows[3] by repeating sacred names which represent the Higher Intelligence.[4]

2. *Contemplation*[5]: One fixes one's attention at the eye center until one becomes aware of melodious inner sounds[6]

3. *Listening to the Inner Sound*[7]: One focuses attention on the inner sounds experienced in contemplation, until the consciousness is drawn up and in, beyond the mind to the source of the Higher Intelligence within. (**This is an advanced technique requiring the guidance of a Meditation expert.)

---

[2] Called "Simran" in Sanskrit

[3] Commonly called the "Single Eye" or "Third Eye"

[4] Beginners can choose their own names; advanced students usually are provided names by a Master Meditator

[5] "Dhyan" in Sanskrit

[6] Called the "Audible Sound Current" or "Celestial Music" or the "Word" or "Logos" or "Holy Spirit

[7] Called "Bhajan" in Sanskrit

Getting Started

BEST TIMES:

The best times are between 3 a.m. and sunrise, when all is relatively quiet and peaceful and when one is less likely to be disturbed. Or, upon rising or just before going to bed are excellent times. In addition, one may take a few minutes at any convenient time of the day, if one can find a relatively quiet place.

Even while sitting on the toilet can be a good time to fit in a few minutes of meditation. In fact, *Repetition* (repeating sacred names) can be practiced at any time during the day when one's complete attention is not required to perform a particular task— i.e., when out walking, jogging, on a bus, train or plane, etc.[8] It is also good to meditate for two to five minutes before making decisions, if you are in doubt or do not have immediate access to expert advice. Sometimes you can receive spontaneous insights.

PLACE:

Ideally, one should designate a quiet, peaceful place in one's home in which to regularly meditate. After a while, as soon as one enters that space, one gets in the proper mood or frame of mind to meditate. Otherwise, brief meditation can be practiced in a number of locations as cited above.

DURATION:

Beginners may start with five minutes at a time, gradually increasing the length as one gains proficiency. Advanced meditators are known to sit for two and a half hours or more, per day. The most advanced meditators no longer have to "sit" to meditate, as they have reached a stage wherein, they are in a constant state of meditation in which they routinely hear inside what is called, "Automatic Sound."

POSTURE:

Sit with the spine straight and still, but relaxed, in a comfortable chair (or cross-legged on a cushion on the floor for those who can do it). The object is to be able to sit for long periods of time

---

[8] Reminds you of St. Augustine who implored the human being to "Pray without ceasing".

143

without moving. The hands may rest on the lap or knees. Clothing should be loose and comfortable. Ideally, where possible, the stomach should be empty.

REPETITION OF SACRED NAMES:

Choose three to five names which represent for you "sacred names" of God or the Universal Higher Intelligence (based on your "spiritual" beliefs). Using only one name tends to increase the wandering of the mind. **(When under the instruction of advanced adepts of meditation, the student may be provided sacred names). These names are not and should not be vocally chanted as "mantras."[9] In this system of meditation, no attempt is made to manipulate psychical or physical energy or chakras (ganglion) or engage the senses.

When relaxed and sitting, gently close the eyes. Begin to inwardly and lovingly repeat, (not vocally chant) the sacred names, slowly and reverently, with the "tongue of thought," i.e., silently within the mind. At the same time, notice or pay bare attention to (without chasing or engaging) whatever appears in one's sphere of awareness, straight ahead in the darkness with the eyes closed. No attention is to be paid to the breathing or any part of the body, and no words uttered out loud, because the object is to avoid any engagement of the physical senses.

Meditation Master Rajinder Singh advises that, "While meditating, we do not hold hands or touch anyone else, as any movement brings our attention back down into the body, distracting us from concentration on the seat of the soul, also called the third eye, single eye, shiv netra, divya chakshu, ajna or aggya chakra, tenth door, or daswan dwar (located between and behind the two eyebrows). We do not put pressure on our eyes. We also do not raise our eyes upwards towards the direction of the eyebrows as that puts pressure on our eyes and forehead and can result in a headache. Rather, we keep our eyes focused gently in front of us and look into the middle of what appears within. We keep gazing horizontally, focusing about eight to ten inches in

---

[9] "Mantras are psychically potent sound syllables capable of influencing the human system"; "Mantras"; _http://www.sanatansociety.org/indian_music_ and_mantras/sounds_of_tantra_mantras.htm_

front of us with closed eyes.[10]

What to Expect

Details of the advanced theory, practice, and benefits of meditation, and the role of a guide in achieving success, are beyond the scope of this booklet. However, a general idea of what to expect in this system of meditation may be helpful to those seeking guidance.

In the beginning, a parade of thoughts may barrage the mind and there may be a tendency to engage these thoughts. However, whenever any thoughts or twitches and itches arise, pay bare attention to them and simply return the attention to the repetition of the sacred names, while focusing straight ahead in the darkness, which automatically puts you at the eye center, the proverbial "third eye." This gives the mind something to do in order to eventually slow it down. Every time you return your attention to the repetition of the sacred names, you are strengthening your meditation muscle. Gradually, you will slow down the mind. No two people are alike, and everyone's history, destiny, and situation is different, so it is not good to compare your experiences with others.

Apart from the drift of thoughts, one may begin to notice complete darkness or lights and colors, the sun, the moon, or stars. Whatever appears, the object is to keep bringing the focus back to the eye center via repetition of the sacred names. If any troubling or questionable images appear, keep repeating the sacred names, which should make them disappear. If this persists (which is unlikely) find/consult a master of meditation to assist you, which is preferable even in the beginning, especially if one expects to progress to the advanced stages. In any case, meditation masters urge you to not share your experiences with others, except for the one who has taught you (as everyone's experience may be different and it is not advised to judge or compare).

CONTEMPLATION (not to be confused with "thinking" or mentalizing):
As one progresses in meditation, one first loses all sensation of the

---

[10] Meditation as Medication for the Soul, Rajinder Singh, Radiance Publishers. Kindle Edition. Lisle, Illinois, USA., (2013 location 3049)

body and the attention becomes fixed at the eye center, between and behind the eyebrows, inside. At this stage, one may experience the melodious sounds, i.e., drum, flute, conch, bells, thunder, humming of bees, etc., and radiant lights, which represent the "Word" or manifestation of the Higher Intelligence. (**Only pay attention to sounds coming from the right side or the eye center, as sounds coming from the left are considered too debasing.[11])*

LISTENING TO THE INNER SOUNDS:

In advanced stages of meditation, the experiencing of inner sounds and radiant lights represents the divine "Yoga" or union with the Higher Intelligence in the form of "divine revelations."[12] These revelations are the divine nectar that guides and protects the meditator in everyday life, in the process of realizing one's divinity.

Hopefully, as one progresses in meditation one experiences a "taste of honey," i.e., moments of bliss and inspiration, more mental clarity and concentration, more calmness and reduced stress, and a feeling of lightness. In order to perfect the process of meditation and experience "divine revelations," one is advised to seek the guidance of one who is an adept at the practice. There's an old Buddhist proverb which says, "When the student is ready, the Master appears," and a Chinese Proverb which says, "Teachers open the door, but you must enter by yourself."[13] ###

---

[11] "Shabd is coming from neither the right side nor the left side; the Shabd is coming from above our head. But because we are in the habit of hearing the sounds from the right and left, that is why we say that the Shabd is coming from either the right or left."; "The Sales Agents of God"; by Sant Ajaib Singh Ji; *http://www.santjl.allegre.ca/sbmag/sbm23-12/qa100280.html*

[12] "yoga is the connection of the soul with its divine origin through revelations. Incessant or "uninterrupted" yoga refers to the stage of spiritual practice at which the connection with the stream of divine revelations has become constant so that it governs all actions of the person concerned"; "The Sacred Scriptures- A Shared Treasure, Circular Seven, January February 2001; *http://centreworldreligions.org*

[13] "favorite quotes"; *Julia Elaine Armstrong's Art Gallery; http://artdanz.com/quotes.html*

APPENDIX II

Fasting: A Spiritual Perspective,
By Leonard Burg - Soul Therapist

Following is a brief overview of fasting, a supreme method of treating and remedying physical DIS-EASE, from both a material and spiritual viewpoint. It includes a bonus section at the end outlining auspicious times for planning and goal-setting during "cardinal points" (key times during the year, months, and days). I speak as a holistic educator and Soul Therapist who has experienced and supervised hundreds of fasts. My purpose is to provide one who fasts—or is contemplating fasting—a spiritual framework within which to benefit from the deeper spiritual purpose of the practice.

Throughout history, saints and sages have taught that the ultimate purpose of human life is to reveal God inside, to experience our divinity as Godmen and Godwomen in the making. It may be true that fasting in and of itself cannot achieve for you the ultimate purpose of uniting with God, nor can praying, going to church or synagogue, embarking on pilgrimages, or engaging in any number of ceremonies, rites, and rituals practiced by religions of various cultures. Fasting, however, is a very dynamic way to heal under normal circumstances, and it can support one's efforts to grow spiritually as there are certain holistic aspects of the practice that are consistent with spiritual unfoldment.

The aim of this article is to help guide you in doing your research and choosing what kind of fast to go on in order to do it more effectively, from both a spiritual and material point of view.

Fasting is Therapy for The Spirit in the Human Being

The word "therapy" means to nurse, care for, or "cure", according to the dictionary. Therefore, fasting can be curative for the spirit. You might ask, "Why would the spirit need curing?" Is it not immortal?"

Although the soul's essential nature is divine, its need of curing assumes that there must be something preventing it from expressing its true nature. The human being is like a lighted bulb which is painted over. Our conditioned ego/mind/body hides the light of the spirit. The curing is the process of chipping away the paint, or impurities, that hide the light of the soul.

Many religious scriptures agree that man is made in the image of God. One way to think about it is that the "man" in human represents the "manna," or "nectar from heaven," or the "mana," the "power, authority, supernatural power" aspect of the human being. In other words, the true "man" in "human" is the spirit or soul, which is of the same essence as God—immortal or Omnipotent, Omnipresent, and Omniscient. However, in the process of "involving" (incarnating) its true nature becomes hidden in the "Hu," the humus or earthly dimension of the human being that returns to the soil upon physical death.

The "hu" in human beings represents the vehicle housing the spirit immersed in a set of causal/mental and astral vehicles. These tend to separate human from consciousness of his divinity, the "human" in human—that is, until the human learns how to reveal God inside.

All the great sages: Christ, Mohammad, the Buddha, Krishna, Moses, Confucius, Lao Tzu, etc., agree that the Lord's purpose for human is to discover how his spirit may find its way back home while still living in the body, and how it may come into the conscious realization of its true nature, which is divine. From this point of view, all sickness is ultimately an extension of lack of knowledge of self as spirit, and lack of knowledge of human's ultimate purpose.

For this reason, the ancient sages have always said that the human being is the "crown of creation." To have this physical body is truly a gift. No other beings of what some saints cite as the 8.4 million species on earth have the grand opportunity that we have—to become self-conscious God-men/women. Therefore, the purpose of fasting and cleaning out this physical body, or "temple," is not just to enhance our body/mind health, its higher aim is to make it a fitter vehicle for us to eventually become a conscious co-worker with God. The question is, how does fasting help to nurture and care for the soul?

Fasting and Attachment

Looking at the etymology of the word "fasting" reveals a clue. Normally, we equate fasting with abstaining from food and/or drink for a period of time. On another level, it is a way of unfastening the attachment of spirit to the body/mind, to support the effort of the soul to fasten itself back to the Holy Spirit and be carried back to God.

The Holy Spirit is called "the Word" in the Bible and Christian tradition (and other names in an array of other faiths). It is what the Lord used to initiate all creation: "In the beginning was the Word." As said earlier, a human being's purpose in life is to reconnect with the Holy Spirit so that it can carry his soul back to God.

This Holy Spirit is within all people, and is fully awakened in the Godman or enlightened saint, whose true identity IS the Holy Spirit, as so many Godmen and women have taught, i.e. Moses, Buddha, Muhammad, Krishna, or Jesus, who the Bible says, was "the Word Made flesh and dwelt among men.") These great redeemers were said to be sent by God to save souls and guide them back home to union (yoga) with God.

Attachment to the body via the mind and senses of perception prevents the soul from experiencing its true nature. This attachment takes the form of all kinds of addictions, cravings, habits, vices; etc. that humanity suffers from in staying blind to its true nature.

Fortunately, as soon as a human being starts to fasten himself to spirit and unfasten himself from that which is polluting him (physically, emotionally, mentally, and spiritually), his organism automatically goes into the fasting mode; it begins to release the associated negative toxins. These toxins consist of poisonous physical substances, emotions, thoughts, and even demonic spiritual entities. Therefore, the aim in fasting is to find a way to aid and accelerate this purification process and be as comfortable as possible while doing so. All supervised fasting programs in one way or another have this aim.

How long one should fast depends on many factors: one's overall health, the daily activities one is engaging in, and the possible contra-indications which you should find out from your study or health practitioner. Some people fast for three days, seven days, or even longer. Some take in only water or fresh-squeezed juices, and some just fast from particular foods or substances, as Christians do during Lent. Others go on what is called intermittent fasts, in which the faster designates certain periods of the day or week as fasting periods. It's left up to the reader to determine what works best for you. In any case, it helps to be able to tailor your fast to your lifestyle, work requirements, environment, etc., in order to save as much energy as possible for the fast to direct to where healing is needed.

I leave up to the reader to research and confer with a health practitioner to decide the kind of fasting you are interested in. The purpose here is to delve into the more spiritual dimension of fasting and how to understand and deal with the side effects that are likely to occur. To get into specifics, let's first define what actually happens during a fast.

Why Fasting works

When fasting, the organism begins to heal itself. It does so by automatically diverting energy that normally is expended in eating, digesting, and eliminating the byproducts of eating, to organs and systems that need healing, emotionally, mentally, and spiritually. The organism undergoes a process called "autolysis," as it feeds off its own toxins, many of which are trapped in reserves of fatty and waste tissues (of which most of us, even the skinny, have plenty).

Fasting is thus a withdrawal of the toxins of living, and, like the drunk or addict, you are likely to crave they very things that have had a toxic effect in the first place, like a drunk or junkie who covets his getting high material the morning after in order to cut the withdrawal. The very thing that is killing him makes him feel better temporarily when going through withdrawal. Thus, when you fast, you are likely to feel the discomfort of withdrawal and a craving or temptation to partake of the very things that your organism is trying to release.

The truth is that you do not experience true hunger during a proper fast. You experience craving or discomfort of withdrawal. Many, not realizing this, stop short the fast because they don't know how to handle the withdrawal properly. They rationalize that they are hungry, or that they are getting sicker, when actually their uncomfortable symptoms are in the direction of cure.

The truest sign to stop fasting is when the tongue clears. You will notice that during the fast, the tongue is very coated with thick mucus (like in the morning before break-fast.) *When you are truly clean, the tongue clears.* Then it's time to stop the fast, because if you don't, the body would feed off its own vital organs. However, not to worry. Very few of us ever fast long enough such that our tongues clear. We stop the fast because there is a time and place for everything. "Spring-cleaning" can't go on forever. We do it in increments. But what if the withdrawal is too uncomfortable? What do we do?

Fasting - Controlled Dis-ease

First, recognize that you are undergoing controlled "dis-ease." You are deliberately deciding to "diss" your "ease," or forego the tendency to indulge in some sensorial but toxic ways of living instead of waiting until the body decides to get sick. You are consciously inducing a state wherein the body begins to release toxins and undergoes a healing crisis to give the organism a chance to heal itself. During this process, many symptoms which you may have suppressed in route to getting sick are revisited. This is called an aggravation of symptoms. This is a good sign, because you now have the opportunity to heal rather than mask the problem. So, in deciding to fast, you are focusing on what you want to do for your soul, the source of life and healing in the body. Otherwise, why should you expect it to provide its soul energy to keep you healthy if you forget its main purpose, which is to re-unite with God? In fact, some saints have said that it may take poverty, ill health, or humiliation to make you turn your attention to God.

Contemporary society tends to push all kinds of drugs and opiates to treat symptoms, but they don't cure, they only suppress. Therefore, while we get temporary relief, we may set up chronic conditions. Sooner or later, these suppressed toxins have to come out if we are to get well.

Much of the elimination in a fast comes from released toxins of medicines like antibiotics, also, excessive caffeine, nicotine, poisons from hormone-injected beef and dairy products, food coloring, additives and preservatives, environmental pollution, and stress-producing toxic ways of thinking and emoting. In this context, all sickness is the organism's effort to rid itself of morbid toxins. The role of the human being is to aid this elimination, not suppress it.

In the process, you may experience what we call "aggravation of symptoms" flare-ups of old ailments. However, if you stay the course, you experience these symptoms in the direction of cure. Instead of suppressing the symptoms, use the following time-tested techniques used by fasters to aid the healing process and make the withdrawal as comfortable as possible, so if need be, you can carry out your normal routine of work or life.

Easing Withdrawal, Discomfort and Aggravation of Symptoms During a Fast

First and foremost, focus on the true purpose for undergoing the fast—not only for health reasons, but to enhance your efforts to grow spiritually. It helps to engage in plenty of prayerful reading of spiritual literature, positive thinking, meditation (and reduction of television, movies, stimulating reading, and strenuous activities).

Following are some specific measures to take in order to ease discomfort during the fast, no matter what kind you choose, because it helps to prevent you from succumbing to the side effects or withdrawal symptoms of the fast, and makes the fast go much more smoothly:

- **During the fast, avoid the following:** sugar, salt, oils, protein, concentrated starches, caffeine, nicotine, flesh foods, anti-perspirants and additive-laden cosmetics, heavy cleaning products, sex, TV, tap water, pasteurized fruit juices, sodas, i.e., any food or activity that tends to enervate or waste precious energy.
- **Instead, if you eat or imbibe "Foods that sustain life,"** that carry the "essential energy" responsible for the endless heartbeat and breath of life:
  - *"Drink" plenty of pure water, sunshine, air, and rest.* Since the vital elements in these "foods" sustain life, they also direct and enhance the healing process.
  - If you are eating at all during the fast, it is best to partake of physical foods that harness the vital energy, such as pure, fresh-squeezed vegetable and fruit juices, and medicinal herbs or homeopathic remedies.

152

- *Limited physical exercise* might include things like yoga, tai chi, qi gong, etc., practices which are like an inner body massage and direct sources of the essential energy and which help ease discomfort from the withdrawal symptoms of the fast.

o **At least one enema or colonic irrigation** (a super cleansing of the colon), for every three days of the fast.

o **Get one or more massages, acupressure or reflexology** treatments. They greatly increase the efficiency of eliminating toxins and circulation of blood, lymph, and healing nerve energy.

o **Daily dry skin brushing with a natural fiber brush.** Start on the left side (as that is where is located the major lymph vessels which carry heavy duty toxins out of the system). With light sweeping motions, start from the ankles and brush toward the heart up to the neck. Do it on both sides. Do this morning and evening. It stimulates the flow of lymph and nerve energy and brings an electrical charge (like rubbing on nylon) to the heart, liver, and other vital organs. It also stimulates circulation of the blood bringing nutrients to the cells and carrying away wastes.

o **Daily hot and cold shower after dry-skin brushing.** The hot water drives the blood toward the heart and the cold water rebounds the blood to the skin surface. The resultant oscillating effect speeds up the blood flow and thus both the elimination of toxins and delivery of vital nutrients to the cells.

o **One Epsom salt bath.** Empty two pounds of Epsom salt (magnesium sulfate) into a tub of water as hot as you can stand it (no soap). Stay in the tub for twenty minutes, and *then get to bed or wrap up warmly.* The salt draws the toxins out of the body. (The skin is the body's largest organ of elimination).

o **Daily deep breathing exercises.** (Oxygen is the breath of life and key to all healing. This is why live foods and chlorophyll-rich foods and juices are so healing).

o **Meditation.** Fasting and all of the above is preparation for meditation, ideally under the guidance of a competent master of meditation. Fasting is tilling and priming the "soil," the body/mind, to enhance its receptivity to the divine revelations that come from meditation when properly done.

In your effort to research various approaches to fasting, I tried to feed you some elements that you don't always find in even the best of books. It is for you to incorporate these ideas as you see fit, or not.

Ultimately, the spirit is the eternal, immortal part of a human being and expresses itself through a series of temporal or mortal bodies, the mental, astral, physical, and etheric bodies. Fasting is one way to help prepare these bodies for humans' attempt to reconnect with their source and reveal God inside.

In many cultures, the times of the year, month, and day can offer more specific auspicious times to fast. The time of the year, in relation to the positions of the planets, has an effect on the bodies of human beings as the spirit manifests in the world. From time immemorial, humanity has striven to live in tune with the cycles of life in order to enhance their growth and development and existence on earth. As a bonus, following is an explanation of fasting in the context of the seasons and cardinal points of the year, month, and day.

BONUS SUPPLEMENT

FASTING AND THE SPIRITUAL
SIGNIFICANCE OF THE SEASON CHANGES

Here, let us distinguish between what I call "horoscopy" (or fortune telling) and a scientific approach to astrology—the school of thinking that uses astrology, not for divination, but to assess the energies available to exercise one's will in navigating in the temporal worlds. These are the planes of existence subject to dissolution: the physical, astral, and mental/causal realms.

On the other hand, enlightened saints, while admitting that oracles may help people to assess the present conditioning his soul is subject to, advise meditation, not oracles, to navigate the spiritual realms beyond the mind because the oracles have no jurisdiction there where direct spiritual experience is required.

The Esoteric Meaning of Astrological Cycles, Planets, and Signs
There are, in fact, many different types of astrology i.e., Sidereal, Medical, Horary, Chinese, Lunar, Vedic, etc., all of which have their specific focus and use. Herein I am referencing the Western or "Tropical" classifications of astrology, not to delve into reading charts, but to illustrate the relative positioning of the planets in relation to the beginning and ends of the four seasons. No matter what system you use:

- On the first days of the spring and autumn, the hours of daylight are equal to the hours of night;

155

- o The winter begins the shortest day of the year; and
- o The summer begins the longest day of the year.

Etymologically, Astrology is the study ("logy") of the astral ("astro") body of human being. The astral body is the body of light wherein human beings have a spirit encased in mental, astral, physical bodies (with an energetic or "etheric" body superimposing the physical body).

The astral body complex is actually a combination of the mental and astral body. The basis of astrology is that by studying the lights in the heavens (the macrocosm), we can gain an understanding of the body of light (astral body) of the human, as human beings are the "microcosm of the macrocosm." If, by thousands of years of study and observation, a planet (heavenly light) seems to correspond to certain qualities and energies, then we can infer that the body of light (astral body) in a human is similarly affected, not by the planets themselves, necessarily, but by the energies they symbolize. If we can infer something about the human's astral complex (which represents his thought/emotional complex) then we can also infer something about the energies and conditioning likely to manifest in his life, because, "As a man thinketh, so is he."

There Are Four 'Cardinal' Points of The Year

In so many cultures, the change of seasons or 'cardinal' points of the year are celebrated as holidays (holy days) and good times to fast or clean out the body and get closer to God. Examining the path of the earth around the sun helps explain this.

Following is a description of the Western, Tropical astrological classifications of the seasons and signs of the zodiac.

1. SUMMER SOLSTICE: The first day of summer in the northern hemisphere, the longest day of the year. The sun enters the sign Cancer. Over a period of 4-5 days, the sun ('sol') seems to stand still ('stice'). It's the point in the orbit of the earth around the sun when the earth reaches an outer point of its orbit, turns, and heads back around the elliptical path around the sun.

156

It symbolizes Shakespeare's *Midsummer Night's Dream*, on the longest day of the year, an excellent time to sow seed thoughts within one's being. It's a sort of 'ovulation' portion of the earth's orbit around the sun (analogous to the lunar cycle's new moon; then the sun and the moon are in the same sign and the soul is thus ripe to be impregnated by the will). It is deemed an excellent time to fast or clean out the body/'womb' to receive the 'egg' (seed thought).

2. AUTUMNAL EQUINOX: The first day of fall: twelve hours of both day and night in the northern hemisphere or temperate zone. It is the day that the Sun enters the sign Libra. It is a time when the seed sown at the summer solstice either lives and grows, or the 'egg' that it failed to impregnate begins to dissolve.

3. WINTER SOLSTICE: It symbolizes the 'Christ-mass' beginning December 21, the shortest day of the year, after which the days (light) start to get longer again—a 'rebirth' of the sun.

   a. The seeds that have impregnated the spirit at the summer solstice now manifest within as divine revelation—a gift of insight within one's being—the true gift of "Christmas." Seeds sown at the summer solstice that have conceived or formed an 'embryo' signaling the coming birth of the fruits at the vernal equinox.

   b. For the inner seed thought 'eggs' that have not been fertilized, the winter solstice serves as a sort of the 'menstrual cycle' portion of the earth's orbit around the sun. It is analogous to the lunar cycle's full moon, when the sun and the moon are in opposite signs. It, too, is deemed an excellent time to fast or clean out the body/'womb' to facilitate expulsion of unfertilized seed thoughts.

4.   VERNAL EQUINOX: The first day of spring. There are 12 hours of day and 12 hours of night in the northern hemisphere. It is the day when the sun enters the sign Aries, a time of the sprouting seed thought which was sown nine months earlier when it fertilized the 'egg' or spirit leading to the birth or manifestation of the seed thought.

Fasting and the Cardinal Points

In summary, the four cardinal points of the year: Summer Solstice, Autumnal Equinox, Winter Solstice, and Vernal Equinox, and the cardinal points of the month and day, are very auspicious times to fast and sow seeds for spiritual and material development.

ANALOGOUS CARDINAL POINTS - YEAR, MONTH, DAY				
Yearly Cycle->	Summer Solstice	Autumnal Equinox	Winter Solstice	Vernal Equinox
Lunar Cycle->	New Moon	1st quarter half moon	Full moon	3'd quarter half moon
Circadian (Daily Cycle) ->	Noon	Sunset	Midnight	Sunrise

In many religions, prayer or meditation is most auspicious at these cardinal points of the year, month, and day (around which many holy-days are observed). They represent times when humanity is better able to receive divine insight or impregnate his body/mind complex with seed ideas that may reap a harvest of spiritual realization.

You may notice that, at the change of the seasons, animals change their coats, plant life changes its flowering capacity, and many people catch colds as the mind/body complex automatically cleanses in preparation for the next cycle. As such, the cardinal points of the year, month, and day are excellent opportunities for you to fast and clean yourself out instead of waiting to get a cold.

BIBLIOGRAPHY

Must Books to Read Re Soul-Over-Mind and DIS-EASE is the Cure

DR. GEORGE C. FRASER
"Click"

In this book, Dr. Fraser writes of the thousands he has helped or been helped by and cites around 600 with whom he has not just connected, but "clicked." In it, he cites ten basic truths geared to master networking and build extraordinary relationships, i.e., "tap into the richest resource on the planet—other people."

CARLOS SANTANA
"The Universal Tone: Bringing my Story to Light"

Like Carlos Santana, yours truly Leonard Burg the author of this book, was a child coming of age in the '60s and, like Santana, rode the lifestyle wave of musical and spiritual stimuli—part of a generation that tripped along, from drug experimentation to holistic lifestyles, from the music of James Brown to Jimi Hendrix, to Miles Davis and John Coltrane just to name a few, and from the church to the guru—a search for spiritual meaning. If you want to penetrate to the souls of many who came through that era, read this book.

ALBERT LOW
"Zen and Creative Management"

The author describes how conflict arises in organizations when people, like animals, act to guard their territory or the space they occupy and attempt to control.

NORBERTO KEPPE, Ph.D.
"Liberation of the People, the Pathology of Power"

The pathology that Keppe writes of, in his own words, "manifests in two basic areas, the first is psychopathology, which speaks about the human being's internal problems, the human being is a victim of himself; and the second, sociopathology, which looks at how the social systems reflect the pathology of the individuals who created them, thereby creating a situation where the human being becomes a victim of a sick society... every person who gains unlimited power feeds his most serious pathological fantasy to such a point that he becomes extremely dangerous to himself and especially to others ... because he is able to give free rein to all of his psychopathology." However, the powerful hate the energy of consciousness. When someone gets power, it's not the power that makes him sick, it just exposes his sickness. "As well, the people that suffer because of this corruption of the powerful also like to imitate them ... it does no good to try to correct the human being while allowing the social milieu to remain the same."

CLAUDIA BERNHARDT PACHECO, PH.D.
"Healing through Consciousness: Theomania, the Cause of Stress"

This book explains how dialogue with clients in a dialectic flushes out the truth of suppressed thoughts and feelings and can lead to remediation of psychosomatic physical symptoms without necessarily needing medicines or hospitalization. The author cites numerous case studies and testimonials.

Claudia Bernhardt Pacheco, Ph.D.
"The ABC of Analytical Trilogy: Integral Psychoanalysis"

A simple, easy to read primer on the science of Analytical Trilogy, an avant garde method of psychotherapy that integrates science, philosophy, and metaphysics. It describes how to apply Trilogy to address Psychosocial pathology and create Trilogical (cooperative) enterprises that facilitate successful collective interaction.

DAVID R. HAWKINS, M.D., Ph.D.
"Power vs. Force—The Hidden Determinations of Human Behavior Fundamentals of the Science of Kinesiology"

The book outlines a means of employing a simple technique via the science of kinesiology to determine 'yes' or 'no' in rating the truth of intellectual positions, statements, ideologies, or the effect of substances like foods and medicaments on one's person. It also presents a scale of consciousness based on the levels at which people exhibit certain types of emotions. A valuable aide to healing practitioners.

Dr. Edith Fiore
"The Unquiet Dead--A Psychologist Treats Spirit Possession"

A book that details how addictive, obsessive, and ultra-depressive behavior may indicate the influence of demonic forces, and how necessary it is to be aware of the existence of entities within compulsive individuals when in relationship with them.

DR. EDWARD E. SHOOK
"Advanced Treatise in Herbology"

A vital resource for any health practitioner, including medical doctors, to use to treat ailments and gain knowledge of the history of medicinal herbs and formulas. The author fully teaches how the organic qualities of various herbs, especially when combined in certain formulas, are useful in the treatment of a majority of common ailments suffered by humanity, in lieu of over-dependence on suppressive drugs. Shook draws from knowledge going back to ancient Egypt (Kemet).

DR. SAMUEL HAHNEMANN, M.D. AND WENDA BREWSTER O'REILLY
"Organon of the Medical Art"

The "bible" of homeopathy, considered to be homeopathy's most important, seminal text, based on the theory and practice of Sr. Samuel Hahnemann, considered to have been the "father" of homeopathy.

GEORGE G.M. JAMES
"Stolen Legacy"

One of many scholarly books that critically document the origins of western systems of knowledge some 5,000 years before the Greeks entered into Egypt for their education, including Plato, Socrates, Aristotle, et al. (NOTE: History reveals that Aristotle believed that some people are slaves by nature, while others were slaves solely by law or convention.) This book begins to put to lie many of the advances of civilization that the western world takes credit for, but that originated in ancient Egypt (properly called "Kemet").

JOHN H. TILDEN, M.D.
"Toxemia Explained"

In this book, Dr. Tilden discusses the chain of causal factors leading to disease symptoms which he described as a crisis of toxemia. He explains how when the toxins are eliminated below the toleration point, the sickness passes and automatically health returns. However, if the cause of toxic buildup continues, the "disease" symptoms reappear. He taught that what creates toxins and blocks their elimination is what he called "enervation," a stressful way of living caused by lifestyle and diet.

JOHN HEIDER
"The Tao of Leadership"

A primer for the leader who wishes to tap more into intuitive faculties in guiding, managing, or directing people. Especially useful in helping leaders to facilitate the development of leadership abilities in the group and among followers. Like John Vasconcellos, chairman, Committee of Ways and Means, California State Assembly said on the back cover: "Tao of Leadership provides the simplest and clearest advice on how to be the very best kind of leader: be faithful, trust the process, pay attention, and inspire other persons to become their own leaders. Its application is universal—for politicians, teachers, parents, clergy, businesspersons, for all of us."

KAROL K. TRUMAN
"Feelings Buried Alive Never Die"

An exhaustive, comprehensive guide or dictionary of psychosomatic correspondences to a variety of physical ailments. It focuses especially on the feelings associated with the conditions—feelings that often people with DIS-EASE conditions find it difficult to acknowledge.

KIRPAL SINGH
"The Crown of Life"

Kirpal Singh is a saint who once addressed the Ninth General Session of the United Nations UNESCO in 1956. He was recognized as a mystic and scholar whose interfaith consciousness was internationally recognized in the 1974 World Conference on Unity of Man. In this book, he does a comparative analysis of the various major religions of the world, and he describes the origins and various forms of yoga as a discipline to maintain and enhance health, heal disease, and grow spiritually.

LOUISE L. HAY
"You Can Heal Your Life"

Landmark book selling over 30 million copies giving the psychosomatic correspondences to dozens of disease conditions. Includes correspondences of ailments to the vertebrae of the spine, and dozens of holistic resources to complement one's quest for health.

NEVILLE GODDARD
"Resurrection"

This book clearly explains how one's thoughts and feelings create one's destiny and how they affect the people to whom one may project these thoughts, and how assuming the mood of the wish-fulfilled acts as a magnet attracting the manifestation of the wish.

PETER TOMPKINS AND CHRISTOPHER BIRD
"The Secret Life of Plants"

This book helps people see the relationship between the environments they live in and how they may be contributing to its conditions based on their thoughts, feelings, music playing, etc. The book explores the rich psychic universe of plants, their response to human care and nurturing, their ability to communicate with man, plants' surprising reaction to music, their lie-detection abilities, their creative powers, and much more. Tompkins and Bird's classic book affirms the depth of humanity's relationship with nature and adds special urgency to the cause of protecting the environment that nourishes us. (Amazon.com)

RAJINDER SINGH
"Meditation as Medication for the Soul"

In this book, a meditation master delineates the manifold benefits of meditation, in relation to its documented benefits for spiritual, mental, emotional, and physical health. He explains how it can be complementary to and benefit professionals and progress in all fields, especially medicine; and he suggests a simple meditation technique that anyone can use.

YVONNE STAFFORD
"From Fast Foods to Slow Foods: How to Wake Up Laughing"

Gary Null, multi-million best-selling author cited this book as, "An excellent first step on your journey to health and happiness". It is ideal for the seeker looking to transition into or deepen their knowledge of a plethora of holistic alternatives available on their journey. It includes identification of healing foods, exercises, detoxification techniques, and a resource guide for what she calls, "Recipes From the Kiss Kitchen."

QUEEN AFUA
"Heal Thyself: For Health and Longevity"

In this book, the author explains methods of self-healing with the help of "Healers" who stress how to utilize life's obstacles for growth and development to overcome illness and benefit anew to experience true healing.

ACKNOWLEDGEMENTS

Recognition of some of the people in my life who share in whatever good I may have done, lessons learned, and support received on this planetary journey.

First and foremost, I want to give praise and thanks to the *Supreme Being* for having given me the gift of life and inspired me to persevere and serve, and the teachings of mystic *Sri Soami Divyanand Ji Maharaj* who initiated me on the path toward Self and God-realization. I also acknowledge: my parents, *Leonard and Anne Burg,* through whom I came into this world and whose guidance I have profited from in spite of whatever travails they have had to endure; my siblings, *Joan, Jennifer, Rodney,* and especially *Allynne* with whom I have traveled this life journey at critical times in my life; my nephews, *Wayne* and *Kyle,* and their wives and children who have reached out to me more than I to them; my grandparents, cousins, uncles, and surrogate parents who looked after me in good and bad times; my wife, *Niiva,* who has stuck by my side through thick and thin as a true soul mate; my children, Kemikaa, Kopavi, Dominique, Raimi, and *Amina* who have been nothing but a blessing in how they have carried themselves and made the family proud; my blended family of *Elaine, Deborah,* and *Jerome* who accepted me and gave me the opportunity to play a part in their lives; my schoolmates at NYU, *especially Kujaatele Kweli, Richard James,* and *Sanyakhu Amare* who have stuck by me, inspired me, and challenged me over the last 50 years; my spiritual sister, *Daya Quander (aka Anjupita Virimo)* who saw something in me and invited me to be by her side in working together during a spiritual renaissance in Harlem and beyond; *Ra Un Nefer Amin (aka Shekem Ur Shakem)*, my first real spiritual teacher who made me aware of the immortality of my soul; *Ms. Ayesha Grice* who had the insight to expose me to my initiation into the world of holistic health; *Mr. Kanya Kekumba* who operated the Tree of Life Bookstore in Harlem, NY where I first "enrolled" in the mystical teachings; *Mr. Bill Burnes* who entrusted me with a tremendous responsibility in motivating and organizing programs for the youths of Harlem; *Bambi Baaba* and the clan of *Sserulanda* whose shepherd-ship taught me much about the spiritual path, personal and collective responsibility, and the taming of the ego; Ms. *Audrey Bloch* who saw something in me and hired me at Pace University, heralding my professional rise in the world of education; Doctors *Norberto Keppe* and *Claudia Pacheco* plus members of the International Society of Analytical Trilogy, who invited and accepted me with open arms into what has been a life-changing experience; *Sharai Robbin*, author and publisher whose course I took that propelled me to write my first book, and who hipped me to the need to add some "ugly" to the story to make it real; and *to the many colleagues, relatives, and associates unmentioned+- who have befriended and mentored me—you know who you are—please know that I appreciate you as fellow travelers on this journey called life.*

BIOGRAPHICAL SKETCH

LEONARD H. BURG - a BRIEF BIOGRAPHY

Over the last 44 years, Len Burg has worked professionally as a soul therapist, holistic health educator, community activist, and higher education administrator. He is founder and president of *www.InnerspireTherapeutics.com.* It helps individuals and organizations unmask and break through hidden inner obstacles that impede progress and success toward well-being and fulfillment, within self, in relationships, at work, and in society.

His spiritual and holistic work has carried him from Harlem, NY, where he directed several community organizations, to Europe, Uganda East Africa, India, and South America where he has organized and supported international initiatives.

In his healing work, Mr. Burg has specialized in helping individuals and organizations transition into healthier lifestyles. He pioneered Soul Therapy, a form of psycho-spiritual coaching and consulting which uproots the emotional/mental patterns and ideas at the root of physical and psychical symptoms. In doing so, he incorporates, 1. **The Science of the Soul**, a scientific approach to spirituality; and 2. the methodology of **Analytical Trilogy**, a novel, consciousness-raising form of psycho-socio therapy that combines psychology, philosophy/science, and metaphysics.

Mr. Burg is also a certified teacher of the basic principles of Analytical Trilogy, accredited by the Brazilian *Keppe & Pacheco College* (www.keppepacheco.edu.br/). Both Soul Therapy and Analytical Trilogy are complementary to and supportive of other alternative and conventional methods of healing that help people commit to well-being regimens and lifestyles.

Len is currently President of *Stop the Destruction of The World North America* (www.stopna.org/), an affiliate of the International Society of Analytical Trilogy (www.trilogiaanalitica.org/en). He has twice presented papers and lectured at its International Psychotherapy Conferences (http://www.icat.ws/videos.php) in Brazil and held English workshops and presentations for its language school and forums in its retreat center in Cambuquira, Brazil.

Mr. Burg was a co-founder and *United Nations* Representative for *A Centre for the World Religions*, the USA branch of an organization which, for eight years, promoted interfaith unity and cooperation and held peace forums and meditations at the UN. At the time, Mr. Burg negotiated its NGO status with the UN ECOSOC division.

From 1998 to 2015, Mr. Burg served at Pace University in New York City, working his way up to Project & Operations Coordinator in the Division for Student Success, responsible for research and projects enhancing student retention. At Pace, he served on the University's Peace Advisory Board and coordinated/ facilitated workshops in Global Citizenship and Justice on behalf of a university wide campaign to incorporate these themes into the curricula and student affairs activities of the University.

Mr. Burg graduated with distinction from Pace University in New York City, earning a B.A. in Psychology and Journalism, with a Certificate in Hands-on Project Management. Most importantly, Leonard has learned at the feet of several living saints and diverse spiritual teachers around the world, promoting the universal brother and sisterhood of humanity. They see and practice "religion" not just as organizations and buildings made of brick and mortar, but as a fundamental process inherent within all human beings, irrespective of sectarian religious beliefs, affiliations or cultural traditions.

Len Burg contributed a chapter, "Profit by Consciousness of Spirituality in the Workplace," in the best-selling book, *The Better Business Book, Volume 2, published by Authors Unite, 2017*

CONTACT:
1 (347) 989-4147; 1 (929) 334-5742
www.InnerspireTherapeutics.com
Lburg@InnerspireTherapeutics.com
Facebook: /InnerspireITI
Twitter: @LenBurg_innersp
Linkedin: www.linkedin.com/in/lenburg
Instagram: www.instagram.com/lenburg_innerspire/

CPSIA information can be obtained
at www.ICGtesting.com
Printed in the USA
LVHW051259100720
660316LV00002B/72